GCSE Edexcel 360Science
Core Science
Foundation Workbook

This book is for anyone doing **GCSE Edexcel 360Science Core Science** at foundation level.

It's full of **tricky questions**... each one designed to make you **sweat** — because that's the only way you'll get any **better**.

There are questions to see **what facts** you know. There are questions to see how well you can **apply those facts**. And there are questions to see what you know about **how science works**.

It's also got some daft bits in to try and make the whole experience at least vaguely entertaining for you.

<u>What CGP is all about</u>

Our sole aim here at CGP is to produce the highest quality books — carefully written, immaculately presented and dangerously close to being funny.

Then we work our socks off to get them out to you — at the cheapest possible prices.

Contents

Published by Coordination Group Publications Ltd.

Editors:
Amy Boutal, Ellen Bowness, Tom Cain, Katherine Craig, Gemma Hallam, Sarah Hilton,
Kate Houghton, Rose Parkin, Kate Redmond, Ami Snelling, Laurence Stamford,
Julie Wakeling, Sarah Williams.

Contributors:
Bridie Begbie, Steve Coggins, Mike Dagless, Jane Davies, Ian H Davis, Catherine Debley,
Mark A Edwards, Sarah Evans, Max Fishel, James Foster, Dr. Giles R Greenway,
Dr. Iona M J Hamilton, Rebecca Harvey, Frederick Langridge, Barbara Mascetti, Lucy Muncaster,
Dr. Mark J Pilkington, Andy Rankin, Adrian Schmit, Sidney Stringer Community School,
Claire Stebbing, Pat Szczesniak, Paul Warren, Anna-fe Williamson, Chris Workman, Dee Wyatt.

ISBN-10: 1 84146 717 0
ISBN-13: 978 1 84146 717 7

With thanks to Glenn Rogers for the proofreading.
With thanks to Jan Greenway and Katie Steele for the copyright research.

Graph of sulphur dioxide emissions on page 10 compiled by NETCEN on behalf of the Department of the Environment, Food and Rural Affairs.

Map of sulphur dioxide pollution on page 12 based on data produced and copyrighted by the Centre for Ecology and Hydrology.

GORE-TEX®, GORE®, and designs are registered trademarks of W.L. Gore and Associates.
This book contains copyrighted material reproduced with the permission of W.L. Gore and Associates.
Copyright 2006 W.L. Gore and Associates.

Groovy website: www.cgpbooks.co.uk

Printed by Elanders Hindson Ltd, Newcastle upon Tyne.
Jolly bits of clipart from CorelDRAW®

Food Chains and Pyramids of Biomass

Q1   Complete the passage below by circling the most appropriate words.

As you move up trophic levels, the organisms are usually greater / fewer in number, the amount

of biomass increases / decreases, and there is a rise / fall in the amount of energy available.

Q2   A single **robin** has a mass of 15 g and eats caterpillars. Each robin eats 25 **caterpillars** that each have a mass of 2 g. The caterpillars feed on 10 **stinging nettles** that together have a mass of 500 g. Study the pyramid diagrams shown and then answer the questions that follow.

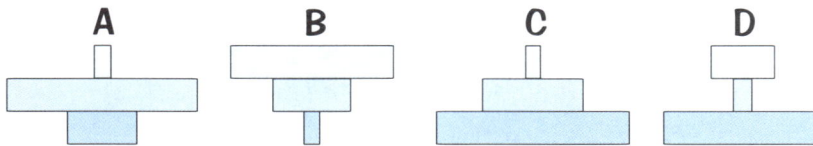

A   **B**   **C**   **D**

a)   Which diagram is most likely to represent a pyramid of **numbers** for these organisms?   ....

b)   Which is most likely to represent a pyramid of **biomass** for these organisms?   ....

c)   Explain how you decided on your answer to part **b)** above.

....

Q3   A **pyramid of numbers** is shown below. Label the parts of the diagram using the following terms:

top consumer   primary consumer   producer   secondary consumer

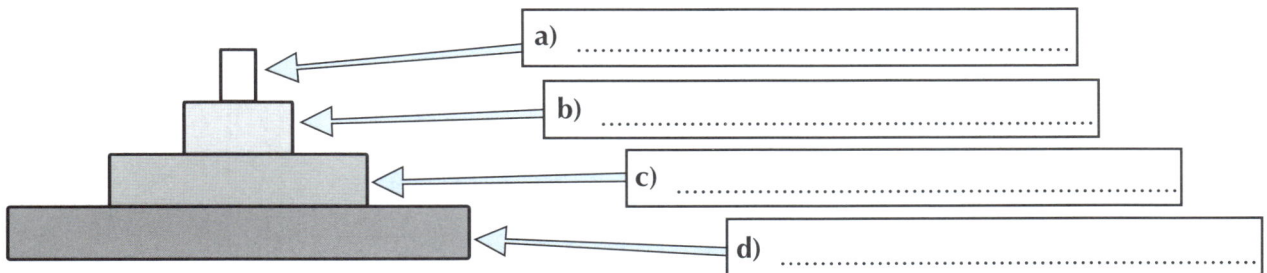

a)   ....

b)   ....

c)   ....

d)   ....

Q4   Place **ticks** in the columns to say which features apply to pyramids of **numbers** or **biomass**. For each feature, you might need to tick one column, both, or none at all.

Feature	Pyramid of numbers	Pyramid of biomass
Values for mass can be shown at each level.		
Nearly always a pyramid shape.		
Each bar represents a step in a food chain.		
Can only have 3 steps.		
Numbers can be shown at each step.		

Food Chains and Energy

Q1 Complete the sentences below by **circling** the most appropriate word each time.

a) Life on Earth depends on **food** / **energy** from the Sun.

b) To obtain energy animals must **decay** / **eat** plant material or other animals.

c) Some of the energy obtained by animals from their food is **gained** / **lost** before it reaches organisms at later steps of the food chain. This is partly because it has been used for **growth** / **movement**.

Q2 Read the sentences below about **food chains** and **energy transfer**. Then tick the boxes to show which sentences are true and which are false.

True False

a) The Sun is the source of the energy used by nearly all life on Earth.

b) Plants convert all the light energy that falls on them into glucose.

c) Energy is used in respiration at each stage in a food chain.

d) For a given area of land it is usually more efficient to grow crops for food than to graze animals for the meat.

e) Animals that have to maintain a constant body temperature lose more energy as heat than animals that don't.

f) Fellsides and moorland are good places to grow crops.

Q3 A **food chain** is shown below.

	lettuce	Caterpillar	small bird	large bird
1	10 kJ	100 kJ	5000 kJ	30 000 kJ
2	30 000 kJ	30 000 kJ	30 000 kJ	30 000 kJ
3	30 000 kJ	5000 kJ	100 kJ	10 kJ

leaf it out

a) Which row, 1, 2 or 3, shows the amount of energy available at each trophic level? ....

b) Circle the answer below that shows how much energy is available to the caterpillar.

5000 kJ   25 000 kJ   30 000 kJ

c) Circle the answer below that shows how much energy is lost from the food chain between the caterpillar and the small bird.

100 kJ   4900 kJ   5000 kJ

Competition and Populations

Q1 Organisms in an ecosystem **compete** with each other for **resources**.

  a) Give three things **animals** will compete with each other for.

    1. ....   2. ....   3. ....

  b) Give three things **plants** will compete with each other for.

    1. ....   2. ....   3. ....

Q2 Indicate whether each behaviour below involves animals trying to **compete** (**C**) or acting as **predators** (**P**) by putting a tick in the correct column.

BEHAVIOUR	C	P
Stags grow antlers during the mating season		
A pack of wolves work together to kill a moose		
A magpie chases a sparrow away from a bird-table		
Spiders spin webs to trap flies		
Lions chase leopards and cheetahs from their territory		

Q3 State whether the populations **in bold** below will **increase** or **decrease**.

  a) A drought dries up a pond where **frogs** spawn. ....

  b) The size of a herd of deer living near a **wolf** pack increases. ....

  c) A disease kills most of the trees in which **cuckoos** nest. ....

  d) A pesticide kills most of the insects that feed on a field of **cabbages**. ....

Q4 Look at the **population graph** for the heron and frog.

  a) Which animal is the **predator** and which is the **prey**?

    Predator: ....

    Prey: ....

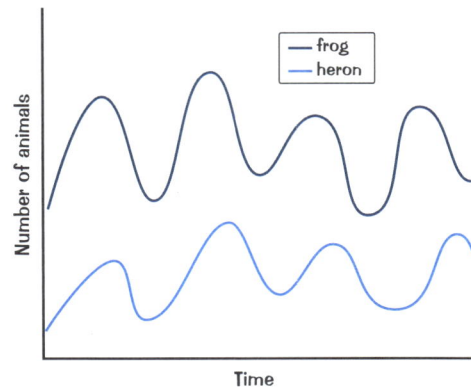

  b) Shortly after an increase in the number of herons, what happens to the number of frogs?

    ....

  c) Name two factors that could **reduce** the frog population.

    1. ....   2. ....

  d) If the frogs run out of food, what is likely to happen to the number of herons?

    ....

Competition and Populations

Q5 The graph below shows how the sizes of a population of **deer** and a population of **wolves** living in the same area changed over time.

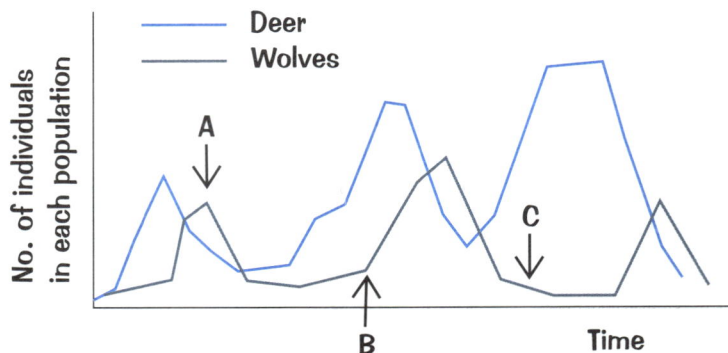

a) Complete the following passage by circling the correct word from each pair.

Shortly after the deer population increases, the wolf population

increases / decreases. The deer population then rises / falls and

after a short time the wolf population rises / falls.

b) **i)** Explain **why** the two populations are connected in this way.

....

ii) What is this **relationship** called? ....

c) At one point during the period covered by this graph, the wolves were affected by a **disease**. Underline one of the options below to show when this was.

At point A   At point B   At point C

d) What effect did the disease have on the size of the **deer** population? Why was this?

....

....

Q6 In Britain, the population of **red squirrels** is declining and may eventually disappear completely. Scientists used a **computer model** to study this problem.

a) State **two advantages** of using a computer model rather than counting squirrels in the wild.

1. ....

2. ....

b) State **two disadvantages** of using computer modelling.

1. ....

2. ....

Evolution

Q1   Dinosaurs, mammoths and dodos are all animals that are now **extinct**.

a)   Underline the correct sentence below.

When an animal dies, it has become extinct.

If you find a fossil, it's definitely an extinct species.

Extinct species are those that once lived but don't exist any more.

b)   How do we know about extinct animals?

....

....

Q2   Fossils were found in the sample of **rock** shown.

a)   **i)**   Which fossil do you think is the oldest? ....

ii)   Explain your answer. ....

....

....

Fossil A

Fossil B

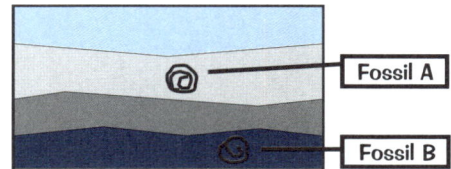

b)   Give **two** ways in which fossils can be **formed**.

1. ....

2. ....

Q3   Choose from the words provided to complete the passage.

cast	bones	clay	shaped	hardens	slowly	rock

In one type of fossil formation, structures like teeth and .... decay

very .... and are replaced by minerals that form a

...........................-like substance .... like the original structure.

In another type of fossil formation, a dead plant or animal is buried in a

...........................-like material which later .... As the organism

decays, a .... is left behind, leaving a clear impression.

Top Tips: Fossils tend to conjure up images of creaky old scientists armed with fossil brushes. But they're the only way we have of knowing about crazy creatures like T. Rex, mammoths, ancient horses the size of dogs and rodents that stood two metres high (seriously).

Evolution

Q4 **A** and **B** are **fossilised bones** from the legs of ancestors of the modern **horse**. Some scientists believe that animals with legs like those in fossil A gradually developed into animals with legs like those in fossil B.

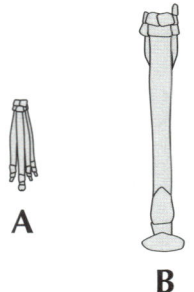

A

B

a) Suggest what advantages animals with legs like those in fossil B would have had over animals with legs like those in fossil A.

....

....

....

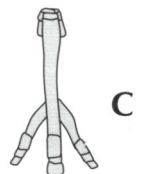

C

b) It is thought that there was a stage in the development of the horse between A and B, during which the leg bone would have looked like C. Suggest why **no fossils** of C have been found.

....

....

Q5 Read the following passage about the fossil record and circle the correct words.

> Fossilisation of dead plants and animals is very **common** / **rare**. This means that
>
> there are **some** / **no** missing links in the fossil record, so scientists **don't** / **must**
>
> update their theories when new discoveries are made.

Q6 Millions of years ago, North and South America were **separate land masses**. Due to movements of the Earth's crust, they then **joined together**. This meant that a North American species of mammal, '**Mammal A**', now shared its habitat with a South American mammal, '**Mammal B**'.

After North and South America joined, Mammal B became **extinct**. Suggest two reasons why this may have happened.

1. ....

....

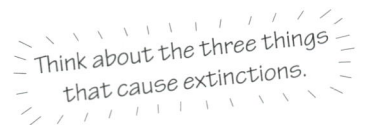
Think about the three things that cause extinctions.

....

2. ....

....

Natural Selection

Q1   Fill in the gaps in the paragraph using the words provided.

Words can be used once, more than once, or not at all.

artificial   rare   adapted   common   breed   die   natural   genes

Some individuals are well .... to their environment. These individuals

are more likely to .... and pass on beneficial ....

to their offspring. Other individuals are not so well .... to their

environment. These are more likely to .... before they can breed.

The useful adaptations are likely to become .... in the population.

This is called .... selection.

Q2   Giraffes used to have much **shorter** necks than they do today. The statements below explain Darwin's theory about how their neck length changed. Write numbers in the boxes to show the **order** the statements should be in. The first and last have been done for you.

[　] The giraffes competed for food from low branches. This food started to become scarce. Many giraffes died before they could breed.

[　] More long-necked giraffes survived to breed, so more giraffes were born with long necks.

[　] A giraffe was born with a longer neck than normal. The long-necked giraffe was able to eat more food.

[1] All giraffes had short necks.

[　] The long-necked giraffe survived to have lots of offspring that all had longer necks.

[6] All giraffes had long necks.

Q3   The **peppered moth** is an insect that is often found on tree bark and is preyed on by birds. There are **two varieties** of peppered moth — a light form and a dark form. Until the 1850s, the **light form** was more common, but then the **dark form** became more widespread, particularly near cities.

**Moths on tree bark in
unpolluted area**

**Moths on tree bark in
polluted area**

Why do you think the darker variety of the peppered moth became more common?

Hint: Use the diagrams to help you.

....

....

Classification

Q1 Circle the correct words to complete the passage below.

> Grouping lots of plants together under the name 'vegetables' is a(n)
> natural / artificial method of classification. A more scientific method
> would be to use genetic similarities / plants' colours to classify them.

Q2 Which of the following is the **best** definition of a **species**? Tick one box.

☐ A group of organisms that look very similar to one another.

☐ A group of closely related organisms that can interbreed successfully.

☐ A classification group containing only a few different types of organism.

Q3 Two types of **goose** found in the UK are the greylag goose and the white-fronted goose. The Latin name for the greylag goose is *Anser anser* and the white-fronted goose is *Anser albifrons*.

a) How can you tell from their names that these two geese are **different** species?

....

b) How can you tell that the two species must be **closely related**?

....

c) What name is given to the scientific system of **naming** species?

....

Q4 When scientists discovered the fossilised remains of the prehistoric animal *Archaeopteryx*, they had some difficulty in **classifying** it. The animal had a structure that suggested wings and feathers, but also a long bony tail, clawed hands and sharp teeth.

a) Why did the scientists have **difficulty** in classifying the *Archaeopteryx*?

....

b) Which features of the *Archaeopteryx* could be described as **reptilian**?

....

c) Do you think the *Archaeopteryx* would have **laid eggs**, or given birth to **live young**? Give a reason for your answer.

Reptiles lay eggs.

....

Changing Species' Characteristics

Q1 A farmer wants to increase the amount of **wool** his farm produces, but doesn't have enough land to buy many more sheep. He decides to use selective breeding instead. Number the **selective breeding** stages in the order that he needs to follow.

[ ] Pick the best of the offspring and breed them together.

[ ] Breed the best wool-producers together.

[ ] Carry on selecting and breeding the best wool-producers for several generations.

[ ] Weigh the amount of wool taken from each sheep and pick the best.

Q2 **Natural selection**, **selective breeding** and **genetic engineering** all change the characteristics of a species.

a) Give **two advantages** of using **selective breeding** rather than relying upon natural selection.

1. ....

2. ....

b) Give **two advantages** of using **genetic engineering** rather than selective breeding.

1. ....

2. ....

Q3 Farmer Norris has three different breeds of cow. He wants to use selective breeding to get the best possible offspring.

Breed A
Average milk yield
Prone to disease
Reasonably healthy

Breed B
Very good milk yield
Prone to disease
Reasonably healthy

Breed C
Average milk yield
Not prone to disease
Very healthy

a) Which two breeds of cows should Norris cross in order to produce offspring with the **best characteristics**? ....

b) Suggest another desirable trait Norris might want in his cattle. ....

Q4 **Tomato plants** are sensitive to **frost**. Scientists discovered a gene in some **fish** which enables them to survive extreme cold. Using **genetic engineering**, they inserted this gene into tomato plants to produce a new variety that is not killed by frost.

a) Suggest one **advantage** of developing frost-resistant tomatoes.

....

Think about the ethical implications...

b) Suggest one possible **disadvantage** of this procedure.

....

Human Activity and the Environment

Q1 The graph shows the amount of **sulphur dioxide** released in the UK between 1970 and 2003.

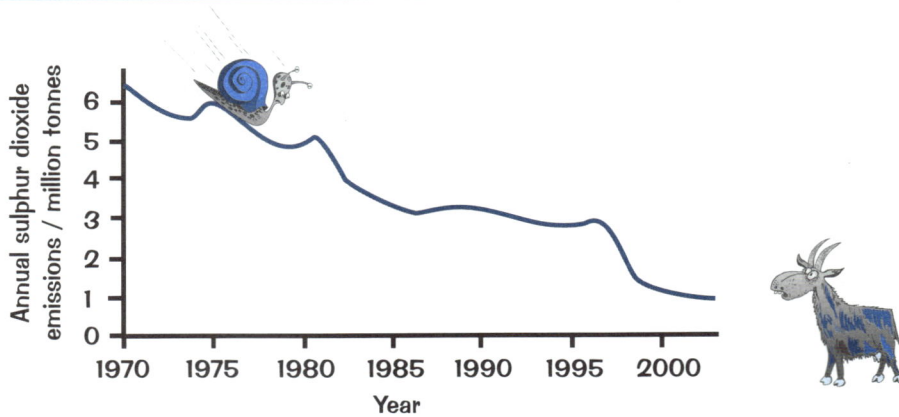

a) In which year shown on the graph were sulphur dioxide emissions **highest**? ....

b) Approximately how much sulphur dioxide was emitted in 2003? ....

c) Name one environmental **problem** caused by sulphur dioxide.

....

Q2 Huge numbers of **trees** are being **cut** or **burnt down** in the world's rainforests.

It's all about CO$_2$

a) State **two** ways in which this deforestation may increase the problem of global warming.

1. ....

2. ....

b) State one other environmental problem resulting from deforestation.

....

Q3 In the list below, circle the letter(s) next to any factors that are likely to lead to an **increase** in the amount of **pollution** generated.

A Industries developing and becoming more industrialised.

B Farmers switching from modern to organic farming techniques.

C Increases in the Earth's human population.

D More widespread use of renewable energy resources.

Farmer Gideon had a brand new combine harvester and he wasn't giving anyone the keys.

E Improvements in the overall standard of living of the Earth's human population.

Human Activity and the Environment

Q4   The size of the **Earth's population** has changed dramatically in the last 1000 years.

a)   Use the table below to plot a graph on the grid, showing how the world's human population has changed over the last 1000 years.

NO. OF PEOPLE / BILLIONS	YEAR
0.3	1000
0.4	1200
0.4	1400
0.6	1600
1.0	1800
1.7	1900
6.1	2000

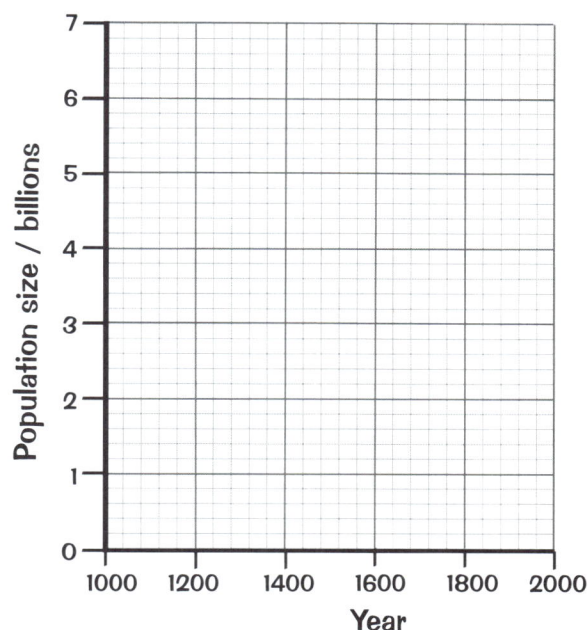

b)   Circle the correct word to complete each sentence.

   i)   The size of the population now is **bigger** / **smaller** than it was 1000 years ago.

   ii)   The growth of the population now is **slower** / **faster** than it was 1000 years ago.

   iii) The impact on the environment now is **less** / **greater** than it was 1000 years ago.

c)   Suggest **two** reasons for the sudden increase in the population.

   1. ....

   2. ....

Q5   In the last 150 years, atmospheric **carbon dioxide** levels have increased from around 280 ppm to approximately 380 ppm.

a)   What are the main processes responsible for the increase in carbon dioxide levels?

   ....

b)   Circle the correct words in the following sentences.

   i)   Carbon dioxide emissions tend to be higher in **richer** / **poorer** countries.

   ii)   Demand for consumer goods is **higher** / **lower** in richer countries.

   iii) The main reasons for increased carbon dioxide emissions are increased numbers of factories and **farms** / **cars**.

c)   Suggest why a richer country might be better able to **reduce** its impact on the environment than a poorer country.

   ....

Human Activity and the Environment

Q6 The map shows the average levels of **sulphur dioxide pollution** in the air in the UK in 2000.

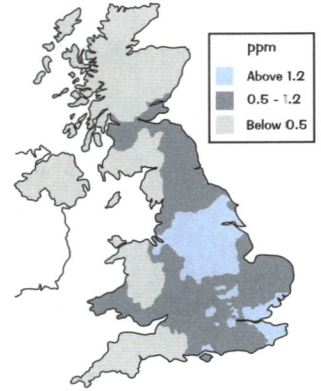

ppm
Above 1.2
0.5 - 1.2
Below 0.5

a) Which of the following is the best conclusion you could draw from this distribution? Tick one box.

☐ The pollution was worst in the north of the UK.

☐ The pollution came from factories.

☐ The pollution was worst in the middle of the UK.

☐ The pollution was a lot worse in 2000 than it was 100 years ago.

b) How would you expect the map to have looked **before** the Industrial Revolution? Explain why.

....

....

Q7 Suggest two reasons why, in general, **economically developed countries** cause more **pollution** than less developed countries.

1. ....

2. ....

Q8 Scientists studied the number of **whales** around the coast of Australia over a period of 15 years. They found that the number of plankton-eating whales was falling and thought that this could be due to the hole in the **ozone layer**.

a) What might have made the hole in the ozone layer?

....

....

b) i) Does ozone depletion **increase** or **decrease** the amount of UV light reaching the Earth?

....

ii) Explain how a hole in the ozone layer could affect the numbers of plankton-eating whales.

....

....

c) Why should the scientists wear sunscreen if they are working outdoors for long periods?

....

Organic Farming

Q1 Use the words in the grey box to complete the following passage about organic farming.

expensive	artificial	traditional	organic	increasing	new
natural		damaging	modern		reducing

Organic farming is a way of .... our impact on the environment.

.... farming methods produce food more efficiently, but there are

some consequences. .... farming avoids this by using

.... farming methods and by not using ....

chemicals. Organic farming is generally less .... to habitats

and ecosystems, but is normally more ....

Q2 Over the last 10 years, much more **organic food** has appeared in British shops.

a) Organic farmers use **crop rotation** to help keep their soil fertile. Explain what this means.

....

....

b) Suggest two reasons why some people **prefer** to buy organic produce.

1. ....

2. ....

c) Organic products are **more expensive**. Explain why this is.

....

d) Suggest another reason why some people **do not** buy organic produce.

....

Q3 For each of the **intensive farming methods** below suggest an **organic farming alternative** and give one **advantage** of the alternative method.

a) **Using insecticides:** alternative method — ....

Advantage: ....

b) **Using artificial fertilisers:** alternative method — ....

Advantage: ....

DNA and Genes

Q1   Ben labelled some sketches of **genetic material** but he made some mistakes. Under each diagram, write down what the correct label should be.

a)

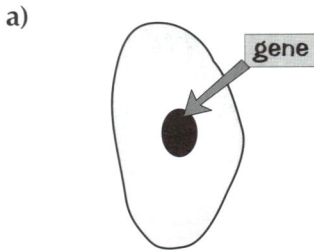

b)

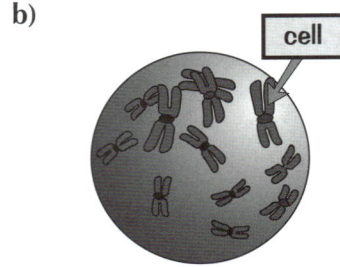

c)

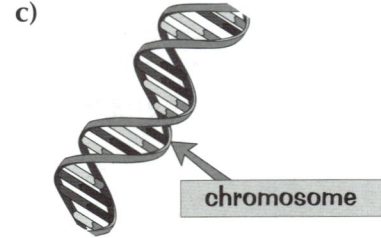

....

Q2   Draw lines to match up the following terms with their descriptions.

a)   DNA   different versions of a gene

b)   Genes   the chemical that genetic material is made from

c)   Alleles   these determine your inherited traits

Q3   Complete the passage using some of the words given below.

DNA	nucleus	genes	chromosomes	allele	membrane

Each cell of the body contains a structure called the ....

This structure contains very long strands of genetic information called ....

These strands are made of a chemical called ....

Sections of genetic material that control different characteristics are called ....

Q4   Tick the correct boxes to show whether each statement is **true** or **false**.   **True False**

a)   Human body cells contain 44 chromosomes.   ☐ ☐

b)   Chromosomes are long lengths of DNA coiled up.   ☐ ☐

c)   Human body cells contain two number 19 chromosomes.   ☐ ☐

d)   All species have the same number of chromosomes.   ☐ ☐

Top Tips: DNA and genes are pretty important to understanding biology — they control everything a cell does and the characteristics that will be passed on from parents to kids. Make sure you know that DNA controls the proteins that are made, and the proteins control what the cell does.

Asexual Reproduction

Q1   Draw lines to match each of the terms below with its description.

Asexual

Clones

Mitosis

Reproduction

Genetically identical individuals.

A type of cell division that produces genetically identical cells.

The process used to produce new organisms.

The type of reproduction where there is only one parent.

Q2   Name one organism that can **reproduce asexually**.

....

Q3   **Diagram 1** shows a cell that is **about to divide** by **mitosis**. Two pairs of chromosomes are shown. Complete **Diagram 2** to show how the chromosomes would appear just before the cell has divided completely.

Diagram 1

Diagram 2

Q4   Arrange these events in **mitosis** in the correct order by numbering the boxes 1-5.

☐   The DNA copies itself before it coils up and forms double-armed chromosomes.

☐   The cell divides and the DNA uncoils.

☐   The arms of each chromosome are pulled apart.

☐   The chromosomes line up in the centre of the cell.

☐   New membranes form around the cell nuclei.

B1a Topic 2 — Genes

Sexual Reproduction and Variation

Q1   Sexual reproduction creates **variation**.

Name two processes involved in sexual reproduction that create variation.

1. ....

2. ....

Q2   Complete the passage below using the words given.

Words can be used more than once.

gametes	egg	reproductive cells	full
sperm	all	both	half	one

The offspring inherit genetic material from .... parent(s) in sexual reproduction. They will have features from .... parent(s).

The production of .... creates genetic variation.

In males these are the .... cells. In females these

are the .... cells.

They are formed in the ovaries or testes from ....

These cells split into two twice to form gametes. Gametes contain

.... the full amount of chromosomes.

The mixture of chromosomes in each gamete creates variation.

Q3   Circle the correct words in each statement below to complete the sentences.

a)   Sexual reproduction involves **one** / **two** individual(s).

b)   The cells that are involved in asexual reproduction are called **parent cells** / **gametes**.

c)   In sexual reproduction the sperm cell contains **the same number of** / **half as many** chromosomes as the fertilised egg.

d)   **Asexual** / **Sexual** reproduction creates offspring with different characteristics to the parent(s).

e)   **Asexual** / **Sexual** reproduction produces more variation than **asexual** / **sexual** reproduction.

Top Tips: Sexual reproduction is a pretty tricky subject. Just remember, there are two main steps — forming gametes and fertilisation. This type of cell division always creates offspring that are genetically different from both parents.

Sexual Reproduction and Variation

Q4 The diagram shows a human **sperm** and **egg** cell combining, and the **fertilised egg** cell dividing.

a) Write numbers on the nuclei of each cell to show how many **chromosomes** each contains.

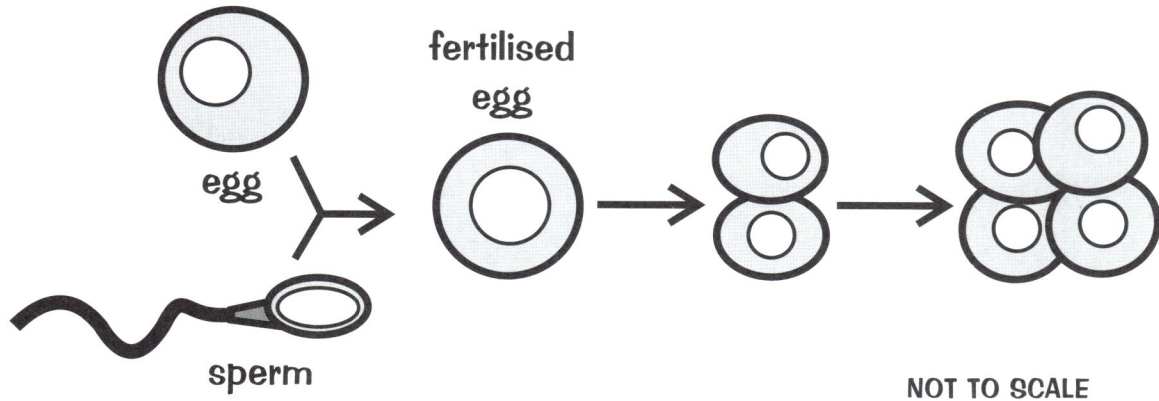

b) What type of cell division occurs after the egg is fertilised?

....

Q5 Circle the correct words in each passage below to complete the sentences.

a) Fertilisation is the fusion of **gametes** / **body cells** to form a zygote.

Offspring produced by sexual reproduction have features of both parents because the offspring inherit **genetic material** / **reproductive cells** from both parents at fertilisation.

b) Fertilisation **leads** / **doesn't lead** to even more genetic variation. Each new individual gets **the same** / **a mixture of** alleles from the father and the mother.

Q6 Tick the correct columns to identify the features of each type of reproduction.

FEATURE	SEXUAL	ASEXUAL
There is only one parent		
Offspring has a different genetic make-up to the parent		
Offspring are called clones		
Gametes are produced in this type of reproduction		

B1a Topic 2 — Genes

Mutations and Genetic Disorders

Q1   Complete the following sentences by circling the correct words.

A mutation in your genetic material can lead to **a genetic disorder** / **an infectious disease**.

Genetic disorders **can** / **cannot** be inherited.

Q2   Circle any of the following that are thought to increase the chance of mutation.

Mutagens

Ultraviolet light

Carbon dioxide

Nuclear radiation

Radio waves

X-rays

Q3   Complete the passage using the words given below.

reproductive	multiply	invade	cancer	genetic disorder

If a mutation occurs in a .... cell, the offspring might develop

abnormally, die or suffer from a ....

If a mutation occurs in a body cell, the mutant cell may start to

.... in an uncontrolled way and .... other parts of

the body — this is called ....

Q4   Give an example of how a mutation can be **beneficial**.

....

Q5   Tick the correct boxes to show whether the following statements are **true** or **false**.

True False

a) Mutations are always harmful.   ☐   ☐

b) Mutations can occur spontaneously.   ☐   ☐

c) Mutations occurring in body cells are passed on to offspring.   ☐   ☐

d) Cigarette smoke contains mutagens.   ☐   ☐

e) Mutations can cause genetic variation.   ☐   ☐

Gene Therapy

Q1 Circle the correct word in each pair to complete the sentences below.

> Gene therapy may be used to treat **infectious** / **genetic** diseases.
> Gene therapy works by inserting a functioning **allele** / **chromosome** into the affected cells. Gene therapy aims to treat the **symptoms** / **causes** of a disease. It can already be used to provide a **temporary** / **permanent** cure for some diseases, and there are high hopes for its future potential.

Q2 Decide whether each of the following statements is **true** or **false**.

		True	False
a)	Cystic fibrosis affects about 1 in 2500 people in the UK.	☐	☐
b)	Cystic fibrosis causes problems with the respiratory and digestive systems.	☐	☐
c)	Some people have genes that make them more likely to get some types of cancer.	☐	☐
d)	A tumour is caused by cells dividing and growing out of control.	☐	☐
e)	A person who has had gene therapy has no risk of developing cancer.	☐	☐

Q3 Some types of **cancer**, e.g. breast cancer, often **run in families**.

a) Explain what this shows about the disease.

....

b) Circle the reason(s) why scientists can't currently use gene therapy to prevent breast cancer.

The genetic material in cells in the breast area cannot be altered.

We don't know exactly which alleles are involved in cancer.

It is hard to target working genes to cells in the breast area.

c) If a patient was treated using gene therapy to reduce their chances of getting breast cancer, might this genetic benefit be passed on to any children they had later? Explain your answer.

....

....

Top Tips: Gene therapy is pretty cutting-edge stuff and it's only in the early stages so it's all new and exciting. But remember, due to the complexity of genetic disorders, gene therapy might only be suitable for the treatment of certain diseases. So it might not turn out to be as amazing as it seems.

The Human Genome Project

Q1 Decide whether the following statements about the **human genome** are **true** or **false**.

True False

a) The aim of the Human Genome Project was to find all of the 25 000 or so human genes. ☐ ☐

b) Human cells have 23 pairs of chromosomes. ☐ ☐

c) Scientists now know the function of every one of the human genes. ☐ ☐

Q2 The Human Genome Project could lead to big improvements in **medical treatment** and **forensic science**.

a) Explain how information about which genes predispose people to which diseases could be used to:

   i) **prevent** diseases.

   ....

   ....

   ii) make **diagnosis** more accurate.

   ....

   ....

b) Complete the passage below using words from the box.

appearance	fingerprint	racial background	personality

A DNA .... can be made from biological material found at a crime scene. At the

moment DNA can only tell us about the .... of a suspect. With

advances in genetics it may be possible to figure out a suspect's .... from DNA.

Q3 Soon it may be possible to test a person's DNA to find out if they are likely to suffer from heart disease. Marco's genotype makes it likely that he will suffer from **heart disease** at an early age. Explain how it could have a **negative effect** on Marco if this fact was made available to:

a) an **employer** who was about to offer him a job.

....

....

b) an **insurance company** who were about to give him life insurance.

....

....

c) Marco himself.

....

B1a Topic 2 — Genes

Cloning

Q1   Draw lines to match each of the 'cloning terms' below with its meaning.

clone

enucleation

embryo

A developing fertilised egg.

An organism that is genetically identical to another.

Removal of the nucleus from a cell.

Q2   The diagram shows a **procedure** that can be used to **clone** a sheep.

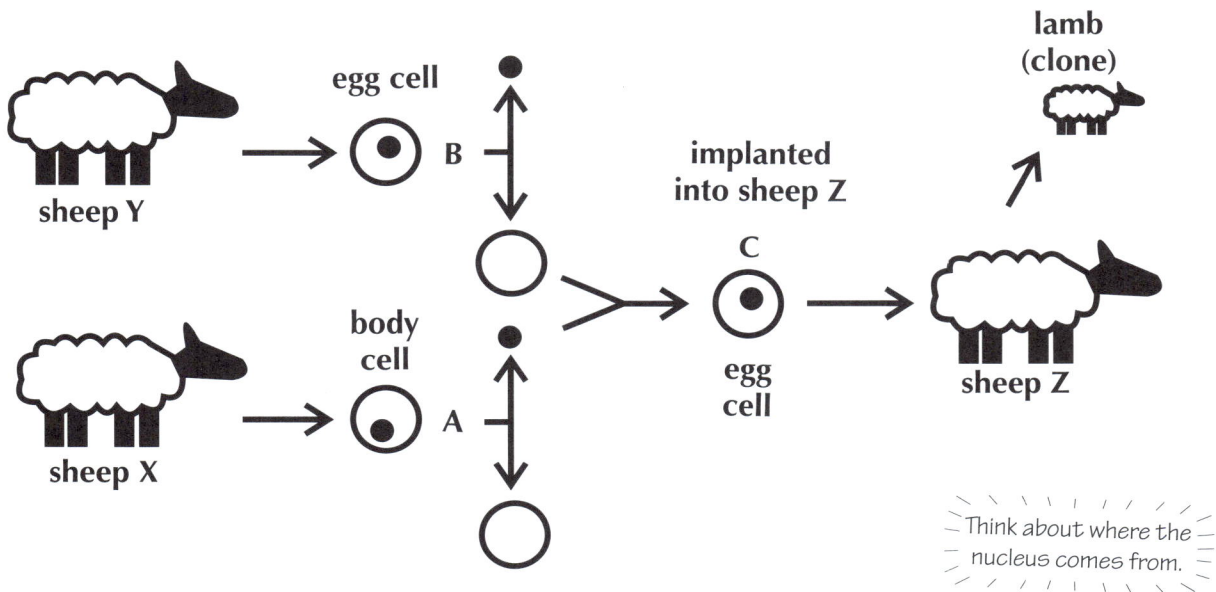

Think about where the nucleus comes from.

a)   **i)**   In the diagram which cell, **A or B**, is **genetically identical** to cell **C**? ....

   ii)   Explain your answer.

   ....

   ....

b)   **i)**   Which of the sheep (X, Y or Z) will the clone be genetically identical to? ....

   ii)   Explain your answer.

   ....

   ....

Cloning

Q3 There are two main types of cloning — **reproductive** and **therapeutic**. Decide whether each of these statements applies to reproductive cloning, therapeutic cloning or both.

Produces genetically identical cells.

Clones are allowed to grow into a whole organism.

May be used in growing organs for transplant.

Depends upon cells dividing by mitosis.

Clones develop from embryonic stem cells.

Reproductive

Therapeutic

Both

Billy...?

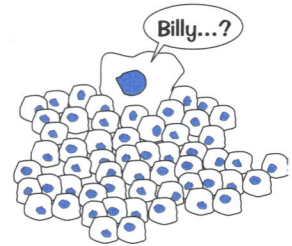

Q4 Complete the passage below using the words given to describe **ethical** issues involved in using **cloning**.

live	destroyed	failures	unnatural
therapeutic	earliest		aborted

In .... cloning unused embryos are ....

There is an argument that even the .... embryos have a

right to ....

Reproductive cloning is also very controversial because if it is attempted there

might be many .... This may lead to severely disabled children

being born or .... Some of the problems associated with

cloning humans would not be known until it's actually carried out.

Some people think any form of cloning is wrong because the process is

....

Top Tips: Hmmm, cloning. It's **always** in the news, with various mad scientists regularly claiming to be about to clone the first human. You have to take this type of story with a pinch of salt though, because the media often aren't too keen on letting the **facts** get in the way of a **good story**.

Mixed Questions — B1a Topics 1 & 2

Q1 In the Arctic, the **lemming** is prey for the **Arctic fox**.

a) The Arctic fox is adapted for the cold Arctic conditions, e.g. it has thick white fur for insulation and camouflage. Explain how **natural selection** has led to adaptations such as these becoming widespread in the Arctic fox population.

....

....

b) The food chain is: **vegetation → lemmings → Arctic fox**

   i) In the box, label each stage of the **pyramid of biomass** with the correct organism for the food chain.

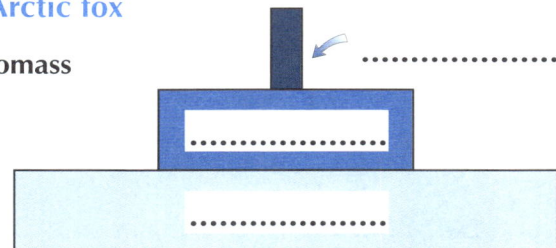

....

....

....

   ii) Give one way that energy can be **lost** from the food chain.

....

   iii) Circle the factors that could cause the Arctic fox population to **decrease**.

   Decreased competition.   Disease   An increase in the number of lemmings.   A decrease in vegetation.

   An increase in vegetation.   Increased competition.   A decrease in the number of lemmings.

c) Use the **binomial system** to write down the scientific name of the Arctic fox. (Order *Carnivora*, family *Canidae*, genus *Alopex*, species *lagopus*.)

....

Q2 Both the **human population** and the global level of **development** are increasing rapidly.

a) These changes are affecting the environment. The release of CFCs is damaging the environment by **thinning** the **ozone layer**. What impact does this have on humans?

....

....

b) Give **two** other ways that the increasing human population is negatively affecting the environment.

   1. ....

   2. ....

c) Many people believe that converting from intensive farming to **organic farming** is one way we can **reduce** our impact on the environment. Outline the principles of organic farming.

....

....

Mixed Questions — B1a Topics 1 & 2

Q3 Fiona says, "**All** organisms contain some **DNA** from their **father** and some DNA from their **mother**."

a) Explain why Fiona's statement is **incorrect**, including an example.

....

Offspring produced by asexual reproduction have an exact copy of their parent's genetic material.

....

....

b) Clones are genetically identical organisms.
Outline one **ethical** concern with reproductive cloning of mammals.

....

....

c) Explain why organisms that reproduce **sexually** contain DNA from both their parents.

....

....

Q4 Ben has **cystic fibrosis**. Cystic fibrosis is a genetic disease caused by a **faulty allele**.

Mitosis produces new body cells.

a) When Ben's body produces new cells for growth and repair, will they contain the faulty allele? Explain your answer.

....

....

b) Fill in the gaps in the passage below using the correct words to show how **gene therapy** could potentially be used to treat Ben's condition.

| lungs | genome | virus | breast | cell | bacteria | gene |

A healthy copy of the .... could be inserted into the

cells in his .... using a ....

c) Ben's faulty allele is due to a change in his genetic material.
What is the name given to a change in DNA?

....

d) The Human Genome Project is increasing our understanding of genetic disorders.
Roughly how many gene are there thought to be in human DNA? Circle the right answer.

50000   46   2500   25000   23

B1a Topic 2 — Genes

The Nervous System

Q1 Complete the following passage by choosing the correct words from the box.

motor	effectors	neurones	sensory	glands	electrical

Nerve cells (.....................) transmit .... impulses from our sense organs to

the CNS. Messages from the CNS are sent to ...., which are muscles or

.... The impulses are carried along .... and .... neurones.

Q2 Which of the following is **not** an example of a **stimulus**? Circle your answer.

hearing   chemical   pressure   change in body position   change in temperature

Q3 In each sentence below, underline the **sense organ** involved and write down the **type of receptor** that is detecting the stimulus.

a) Tariq puts a piece of lemon on his tongue. The lemon tastes sour.

....

b) Siobhan wrinkles her nose as she smells something unpleasant in her baby brother's nappy.

....

c) Lindsey covers her eyes when she sees the man in the mask jump out during a scary film.

....

d) Xabi's ears were filled with the sound of the crowd cheering his outstanding goal.

....

Q4 Give two reasons why it is important for animals to be able to **detect changes** in their surroundings (stimuli).

1. ....

....

2. ....

....

The Nervous System

Q5 Explain why a man with a **damaged spinal cord** may not be able to feel someone touching his toe.

....

....

The spinal cord contains neurones that carry impulses to the brain.

Q6 Some parts of the body are known as the **CNS**.

a) What do the letters **CNS** stand for? ....

b) Name the two main parts of the CNS.

1. .... 2. ....

c) What type of neurone:

   i) carries information **to** the CNS? ....

   ii) carries instructions **from** the CNS? ....

Q7 John and Marc investigated how **sensitive** different parts of the body are to **pressure**. They stuck two pins in a cork 0.5 cm apart. The pins were placed on different parts of the body. Ten pupils took part — they were blindfolded and reported "yes" or "no" to feeling both points. The results of the experiment are shown in the table.

Area of the body tested	Number of pupils reporting 'yes'
Sole of foot	2
Knee	3
Fingertip	10
Back of hand	5
Lip	9

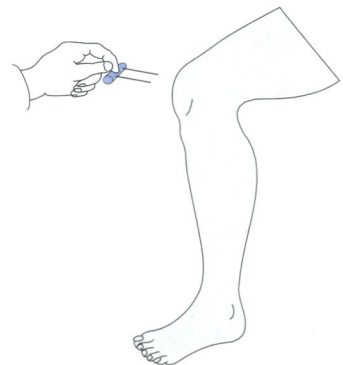

a) Which part of the body do the results suggest is:

   i) most sensitive? ....

   ii) least sensitive? ....

A higher concentration of receptors would make an area more sensitive.

b) From the results above, which part of the body do you think contains the greatest concentration of **pressure receptors**? Explain your answer.

....

....

The Central Nervous System

Q1   Decide whether each of the statements below is **true** or **false**.

                                                                                   True   False

a)   The right side of the cerebrum controls the left side of the body. ☐ ☐

b)   The cerebellum is the largest part of the brain. ☐ ☐

c)   Each sense (sight, hearing etc.) is processed in a different area (or areas) of the brain. ☐ ☐

d)   The cerebrum coordinates sensory information. ☐ ☐

Q2   Label the diagram of the brain using the words in the box.

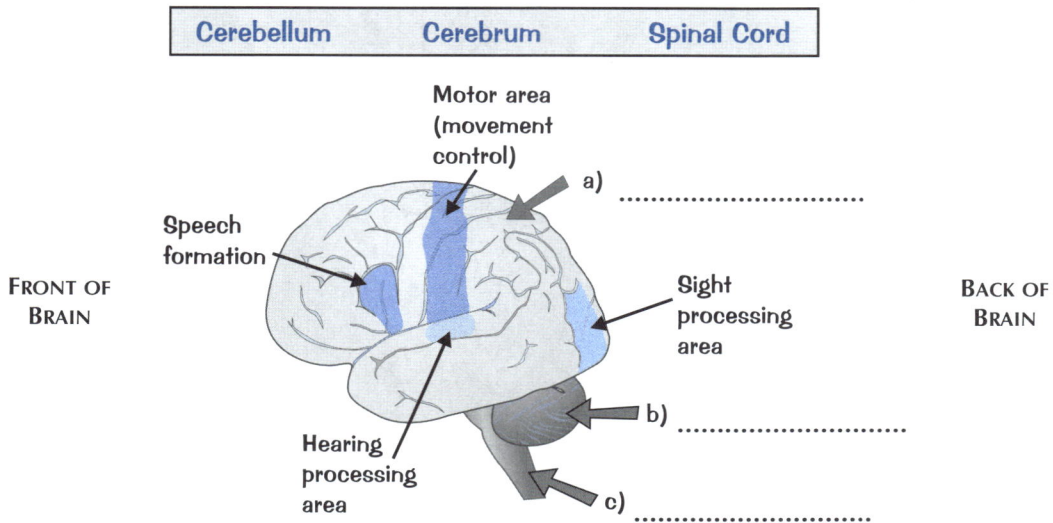

Cerebellum	Cerebrum	Spinal Cord

Motor area (movement control)

Speech formation

FRONT OF BRAIN

Sight processing area

BACK OF BRAIN

a) ....

b) ....

Hearing processing area

c) ....

Q3   Responses to a stimulus can be **voluntary** or **involuntary** (reflex). Circle the correct word(s) in the sentences below.

a)   A **voluntary** response to a stimulus is a response that is **conscious** / **automatic**.

You **need** / **don't need** to think about how to respond.

b)   An **involuntary** response to a stimulus is a response that is **conscious** / **automatic**.

You **need** / **don't need** to think about how to respond.

Q4   How can knowledge about the areas of the brain help diagnose **brain damage**?

....

....

....

Top Tips: An adult human brain weighs about 1.4 kg — it's an incredibly complicated system of about 100 billion nerves, and if you could unravel them all, they'd stretch for more than 150 000 km. You don't need to know any of that, but I reckon it's pretty interesting stuff...

The Central Nervous System

Q5 Tom and Jane did an experiment on **reaction times**. Tom held a ruler vertically between Jane's thumb and forefinger, with her forefinger in line with the zero mark.
Tom dropped the ruler **without warning** and measured how far it fell before Jane caught it.
They repeated their experiment five times. The measurements are shown in the table below.

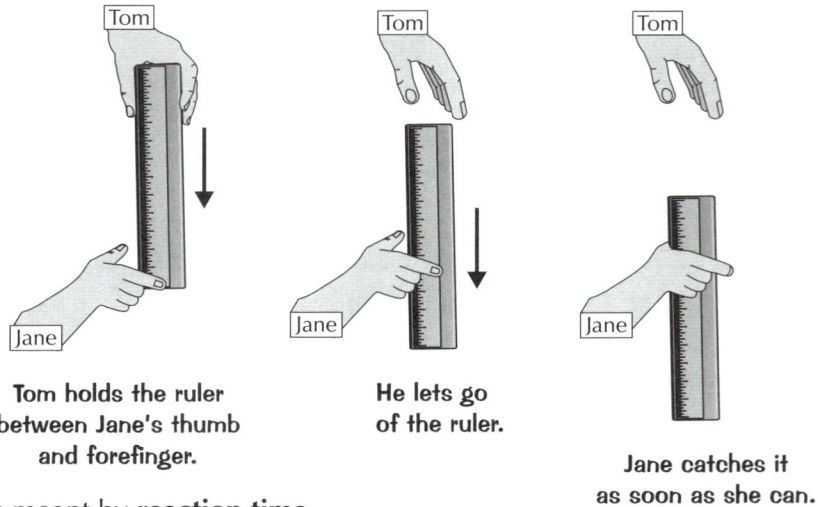

Tom holds the ruler
between Jane's thumb
and forefinger.

He lets go
of the ruler.

Jane catches it
as soon as she can.

a) Explain what is meant by **reaction time**.

....

....

Jane's attempts	Measurements (cm)
1	13
2	26
3	20
4	12
5	9

b) Calculate Jane's **average** measurement using the data provided in the table.

....

c) Suggest two reasons why Jane's results varied so much.

1. ....

....

2. ....

....

d) They also carried out the experiment with Jane dropping the ruler and Tom catching it. Tom's average measurement was 20 cm.
Who had the quicker reaction time?

The less distance the ruler fell the quicker the reaction time.

....

e) Tom and Jane repeated their experiment five times each. Why did they do this?

....

Reflex Responses

Q1   Complete the following passage by choosing the correct words from the box.

a receptor	neurones	an effector	CNS

A reflex arc is a set of .... that carry information from

.... to ...., via the ....

This produces an automatic response to a stimulus.

Q2   Circle the correct answers to complete the following sentences.

a)   Reflexes happen more **quickly** / **slowly** than considered (voluntary) responses.

b)   The **vertebrae** / **spinal cord** can coordinate a reflex response.

c)   The main purpose of a reflex is to **protect** / **display** the body.

d)   Reflexes happen **with** / **without** conscious thought.

Q3   Reflex actions are **automatic**.

Give an example of how reflex actions could save your body from injury.

....

....

....

Q4   Put the steps in order (1-5) to describe the **reflex response** when a ball flies at your head.

☐ An impulse is sent along a motor neurone to the muscles in your neck, shoulder and stomach.

☐ You duck and avoid the ball.

☐ The light receptors in your eyes detect the ball.

☐ In the CNS the sensory neurone passes on the message to a relay neurone which relays the impulse to a motor neurone.

☐ An impulse is sent along a sensory neurone to the CNS.

Reflex Responses

Q5 When you touch something hot with a finger you **automatically** pull the finger away.
The diagram shows some parts of the nervous system involved in this **reflex action**.

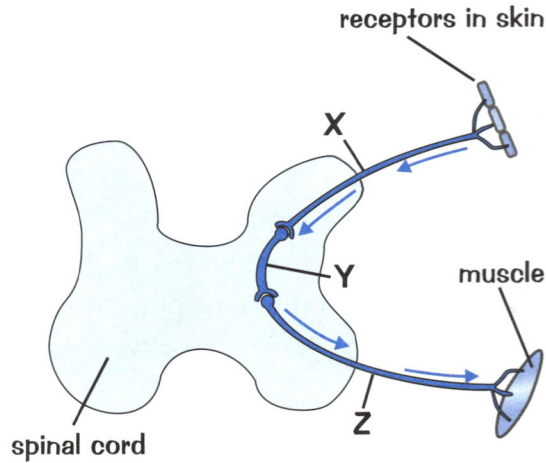

receptors in skin

X

Y

muscle

Z

spinal cord

a) Match the following to the correct letter shown on the diagram.

X		relay neurone
Y		motor neurone
Z		sensory neurone

b) Complete the sentence.

In this reflex action the muscle acts as the ....

Q6 Give another example of a stimulus that might cause a reflex reaction. What might the response be?

stimulus: ....

response: ....

Q7 Why is a **reflex** response faster than a **voluntary** response?

Think about whether the impulse is 'processed'.

....

....

....

Top Tips: Reflexes are really fast — that's the whole point of them. And the fewer synapses the signals have to cross, the faster the reaction. Doctors test people's reflexes by tapping below their knees to make their legs jerk. This reflex takes less than 50 milliseconds as only two synapses are involved.

Examples of Reflex Actions

Q1 From the list below, underline any actions that are examples of **reflex actions**.

Pupil getting smaller in bright light

Sneezing

Pulling your hand away from something hot

Wiping a piece of dirt from your eye

Blinking when something flies at your face

Q2 Look carefully at the diagrams showing two different **eyes** below.

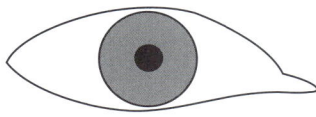
Eye A

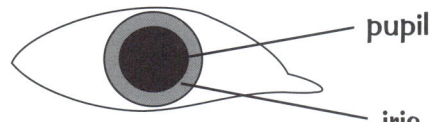
pupil

iris

Eye B

a) Describe the difference you can see in the appearance of the two eyes.

....

....

b) Which diagram do you think shows an eye in bright light? Explain your answer.

....

....

....

c) Explain why it is an advantage to have this type of response controlling the action of the eye.

....

Think about why you shouldn't look straight at the Sun.

....

....

Q3 Read the following passage about accommodation and circle the correct word in each pair.

When you look at an object, light / distance receptors send a message along a motor / sensory

neurone to your brain. Your brain works out if the object is in focus and if it's not it sends a message

along a motor / sensory neurone to the ciliary muscles, which control the thickness of the lens. If the

object is far away, the ciliary muscles contract / relax, and the suspensory ligaments tighten / slacken.

The lens will be thin / fat. The opposite happens for near objects.

The Blood

Q1   **Oxygen** is carried around the body in the **blood**.

> The job of the **red** / **white** blood cells is to carry oxygen around the body.
> They contain haemoglobin, which contains **a lot of** / **no** iron. Oxygen is
> obtained from the **body cells** / **lungs** and released at the **body cells** / **lungs**.

Q2   **Platelets** are small fragments of cells.

   a)   What is the main function of platelets?

   ....

   b)   What effect would a lack of platelets have on the body?

   ....

Q3   **White blood cells** defend the body against **disease**.

   a)   State two ways in which white blood cells can protect your body from microorganisms.

   1. ....

   2. ....

   b)   A man was feeling unwell and went to see his doctor. The doctor did a blood test and found that
          the patient's white blood cell count was higher than normal. Suggest a reason for this.

   ....

   Think about when you might need lots of white blood cells.

Q4   **Plasma** is the substance that carries everything in the blood.

   a)   List six substances that are carried by plasma.

   ....

   ....

   b)   For each of the substances listed in the table, state where in the body it is travelling **from** and **to**.

Substance	Travelling from	Travelling to
Urea	Liver	Kidneys
Carbon dioxide		
Glucose		

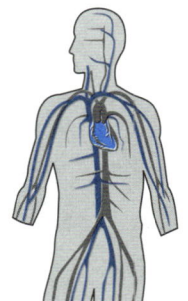

Hormones

Q1 Use the words in the box to complete the passage below about **hormones**.

chemical	glands	blood	target

Hormones are .... messengers. They are produced in

.... and released into the .... They are

carried all around the body, but only affect certain .... cells.

Q2 Match the **hormones** below with where they are **produced** and the **action** they have.

Hormone	Site produced	Action
a) Oestrogen and progesterone	Pancreas	Controls the menstrual cycle
b) Insulin	Ovaries	Controls blood sugar levels

Q3 Hormones can reach **every cell** in the body. Only the **target cells** respond to the hormone, while the others are unaffected.

What **structures** on the target cells cause them to respond to the hormone? ....

Q4 One of the first experiments to show hormones working was done by two scientists called Bayliss and Starling. They knew that the presence of **food** in the **stomach** caused the **pancreas** (a completely different organ) to produce pancreatic juice, but they didn't know if the pancreas was triggered by **nerves** or by something in the **blood**.

When they sedated a dog and cut away all the **nerves** going to the stomach and pancreas, pancreatic juice was **still produced**. Underline the best conclusion based on these findings.

Nerves control the production of pancreatic juice.

The stimulus which causes pancreatic juice to be released is carried in the blood.

Q5 Fill in the table to show the differences between **nervous** and **hormonal** communication.

Properties	Nerves	Hormones
Type of message		
Speed of message	Very fast	
Length of action		Act for a long time
Site of action	Act on a very precise area	

Hormones — Insulin and Diabetes

Q1   Circle the correct answers to complete the following sentences.

   a)   Eating foods rich in **carbohydrates** / **protein** puts a lot of glucose into the blood.

   Glucose is a type of **sugar** / **vitamin**.

   b)   **Insulin** / **Oestrogen** is involved in the regulation of blood sugar levels.

   It is produced in the **pancreas** / **ovaries**.

Q2   Deepa doesn't eat anything for lunch because she is busy. In the afternoon she has two biscuits and by **6pm** she is so hungry that for tea she eats a plate of pasta and six slices of toast with jam. The graph below shows Deepa's blood sugar levels from **12pm** to **8pm**.

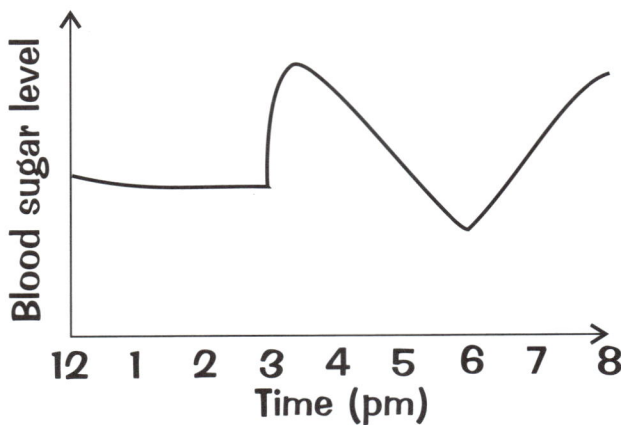

Eating foods high in sugar (like biscuits) increases the blood sugar level.

   a)   What time did Deepa eat the two biscuits? ....

   b)   **i)**   If Deepa's blood sugar level is **too high**, what would her body produce to reduce it?

   ....

   ii)   What effect would this have?

   ....

Q3   Approximately **1.8 million** people in the UK have **diabetes**.

   a)   Complete the following passage by inserting the correct words.

   Diabetes is a disease in which the .... does not produce

   enough .... This means the person's ....

   could rise to harmful levels.

   b)   Which organ starts to remove glucose from the blood when insulin is injected by a diabetic?

   ....

Hormones — Insulin and Diabetes

Q4   Ruby and Paul both have diabetes and need to **monitor** and **control** their glucose levels carefully.

a)   Describe the two main ways that diabetics can **control** their blood sugar levels.

1. ....

2. ....

b)   Ruby injects insulin just before she is about to eat a big meal.   What effect does this have on her blood sugar level?   Circle the correct answer.

It increases   It decreases

c)   One evening Paul goes out for a meal. He has forgotten to inject any insulin, and eats a large meal including a sugary dessert. A few hours after the meal Paul collapses and has to be taken to hospital for treatment.

i)   What treatment would you expect Paul to be given when he arrives at hospital?

Doctors need to reduce his blood sugar.

....

....

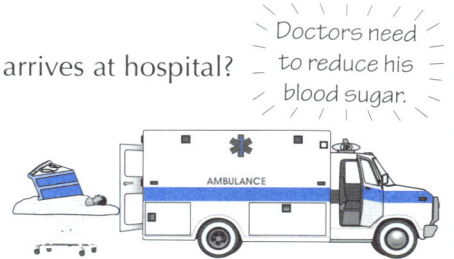

ii)   What will happen to the excess glucose in Paul's blood?

....

Q5   Diabetics used to inject themselves with insulin that came from **cows** or **pigs**. Nowadays, all the insulin used is human insulin, which is made by **genetically modified bacteria**.

Give two advantages of using human insulin produced by bacteria rather than cow or pig insulin.

1. ....

....

2. ....

....

Top Tips: Although diabetes is a serious disease, many diabetics are able to control their blood sugar levels and carry on with their normal lives. Sir Steve Redgrave even won a gold medal at the Olympics after he had been diagnosed with diabetes.

Hormones — Fertility

Q1 Complete the following passage by choosing the correct words from the box.

fertilisation	oral	progestrone	egg	oestrogen

The pill is an .... contraceptive that contains ....

and .... It reduces fertility by stopping ....

production. This means that .... cannot take place.

Q2 Hormones can also be used to **increase fertility**.

a) Name the hormone often taken by women who aren't releasing any eggs. ....

b) Describe a possible disadvantage of taking hormones to increase fertility in women.

....

....

Q3 **In vitro fertilisation** can help couples to have children.

a) Explain how **in vitro fertilisation** is different from natural fertilisation.

....

....

b) Give one disadvantage of in vitro fertilisation.

....

....

Q4 The graph shows the **percentage success rates** of **IVF treatment** for women in the UK in 2002–3.

Image based on data produced by the Human Fertilisation and Embryology Authority: www.hfea.gov.uk

a) What was the % success rate in women aged 35–37? ....

b) What conclusion can be drawn about the effect of a woman's age on the success of IVF treatment? Underline the correct answer.

It's more likely to be successful as the woman gets older.

There's an equal chance of success regardless of age.

It's less likely to be successful as the woman gets older.

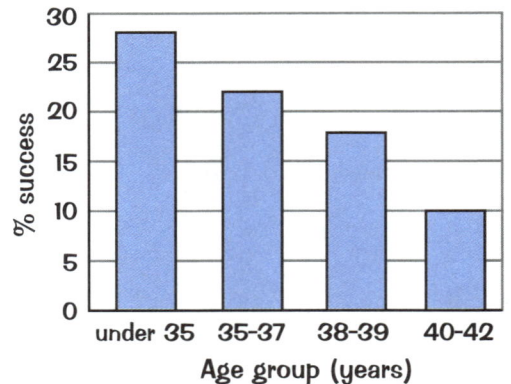

c) Suggest two issues surrounding IVF treatment for women over 40.

....

....

The Body's Defence Systems

Q1 The body has several methods of **defending itself** against the entry of **pathogens**.

a) Below are examples of how some bacterial pathogens can enter the body.
In each case, describe how your body defends itself against illness.

i) *Staphylococcus aureus* can cause blood poisoning by getting into the blood through cuts.

....

....

ii) *Streptococcus pneumoniae* can enter the body from the air as a person breathes.

....

....

b) The sensitive **eye** area is also protected against infection by microorganisms.
Pick words from the list below to fill in the paragraph.

enzyme	chemical	sleep	lysozyme	physical	tears

Eyes produce ...., which contain a chemical called

.... This kills bacteria that land on the surface of the eye.

This is a .... barrier.

Q2 **Lymphocytes** and **phagocytes** are two different types of **white blood cell** that defend the body against invasion by microorganisms.

a) Decide whether each of the following sentences applies to **lymphocytes**, to **phagocytes** or to **both**.

i) They are able to kill invading microbes directly. ....

ii) They are non-specific and attack any 'foreign' bodies. ....

iii) They are able to secrete antibodies. ....

iv) They have receptors which allow them to attack specific microbes. ....

b) White blood cells also trigger an **inflammatory response**. Describe the effect that this has on the body, and explain why it is necessary.

....

....

....

The Body's Defence Systems

Q3 Circle the correct word from each pair to complete the following passages.

Lymphocytes have receptors that allow them to recognise molecules called antibodies / antigens on the surface of certain phagocytes / pathogens. Antigens are substances that cause an immune response.

Some types of lymphocyte secrete antibodies / antigens that latch onto the invading cells and mark them so that other white blood cells can recognise and kill them. Other types attach directly to antigens / antibodies and destroy the cells carrying them.

Q4 Tick the boxes to show whether each statement is **true** or **false**.

		True	False
a)	Lymphocytes attack specific microbes.	☐	☐
b)	Antigens are usually protein molecules.	☐	☐
c)	An antibody for one type of bacteria will latch on to another type of bacteria.	☐	☐

Q5 If you have already had **chickenpox** you will usually be **immune** to the disease and will not suffer any symptoms if you are exposed to the infection again. Order the sentences below to show why this happens.

A You are infected with chickenpox for the first time.

B The white blood cells produce lots of antibodies very quickly.

C You are exposed to chickenpox microbe for a second time.

D Your white blood cells multiply very rapidly.

E Your white blood cells respond and you slowly recover from it.

F The antibodies cause the death of the microbes before you experience any symptoms.

G Some of the lymphocytes that are specific to the chickenpox microbe remain in the blood.

Order: *A* ....

Top Tips: It's really important that you don't get phagocytes and lymphocytes mixed up. Phagocytes are non-specific — they'll attack anything that isn't supposed to be there. Lymphocytes have receptors which mean they'll only attack specific microbes.

Infectious Diseases

Q1 **Infectious diseases** are caused by **pathogens**.
Decide whether the following statements are **true** or **false**.

True False

a) All pathogens are parasites. ☐ ☐

b) Infectious diseases can be passed on genetically. ☐ ☐

c) All pathogens are bacteria. ☐ ☐

d) Infectious diseases are not caused by living organisms. ☐ ☐

e) Pathogens can be spread between organisms by both direct and indirect contact. ☐ ☐

Q2 Some infectious diseases are spread by **direct contact**.

a) Explain what this means.

....

....

....

b) The table below shows some ways that infections can be passed on. Complete the table to show one **example** of a disease that might be spread in each way, and whether it is an example of **vertical** transmission or **horizontal** transmission.

	Droplet infection	Placental infection (from mother to baby)	Sexually transmitted infection
Example	common cold	HIV	
Type of transmission			horizontal

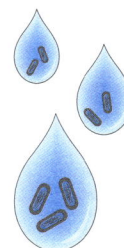

Q3 Complete the following passage by circling the correct words.

Influenza is spread by **vertical transmission** / **droplet infection** — in the same way as **TB** / **rabies**. It's transmitted when an infected person coughs or sneezes near someone. People with symptoms should **stay at home** / **go to work** and use tissues when they sneeze.

Gonorrhoea is passed on via **vectors** / **sexual intercourse**, so an infected person might try to limit their number of **sexual partners** / **insect bites** and should always use **condoms** / **contraceptive pills** if they have intercourse.

Infectious Diseases

Q4 The graph shows the change in someone's **body temperature** during a **flu infection**. Their temperature was recorded at the same time every day.

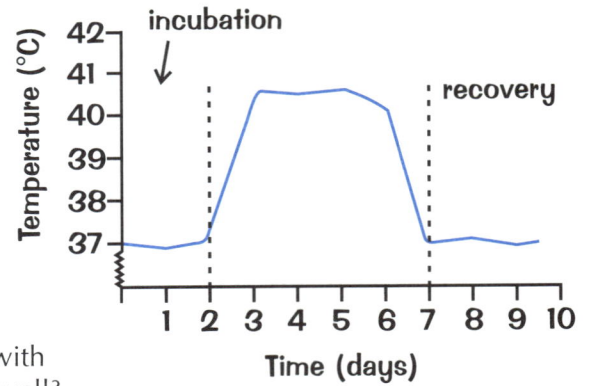

a) What was the **maximum** body temperature during this illness?

....

b) Approximately how many days after direct contact with someone infected with flu might you start to feel unwell?

....

A fever would make you feel unwell.

c) The influenza virus is an example of a microbe spread by **horizontal transmission**. What does this mean?

....

....

Q5 Pathogens can also be transmitted by **indirect contact**.

a) Complete the table on the right by ticking the correct boxes to match the infectious diseases with their carriers.

The first one has been done for you.

Infectious disease	Vector	Vehicle
sleeping sickness	✓	
typhoid		
malaria		
verrucas		
salmonella		

b) Explain the difference between a **vector** and a **vehicle**.

....

c) Match the following diseases to their vector/vehicle, and to how humans can prevent their spread.

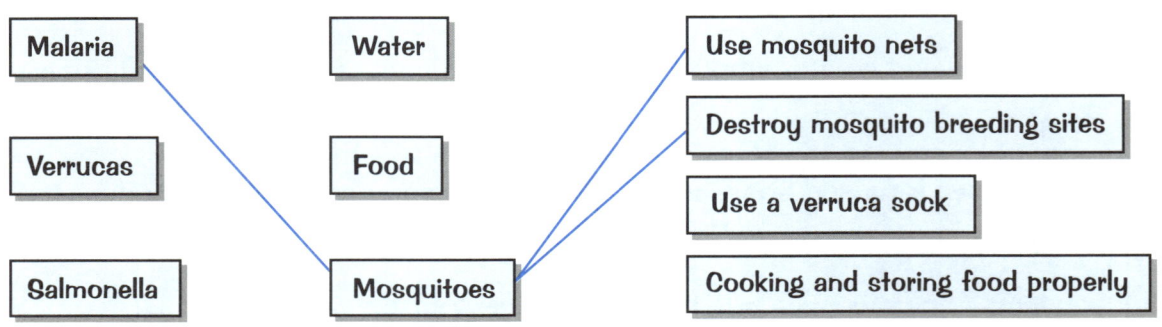

Malaria — Water — Use mosquito nets
Verrucas — Food — Destroy mosquito breeding sites
Salmonella — Mosquitoes — Use a verruca sock — Cooking and storing food properly

TB — Tuberculosis

Q1 Tuberculosis is caused by a microorganism called **Mycobacterium tuberculosis**.

a) What kind of microorganism is *Mycobacterium tuberculosis*? Tick the correct answer.

☐ Fungus   ☐ Bacterium   ☐ Virus

b) How is this organism **spread** from a disease sufferer to a new host? Circle one of the following:

insect vector   droplet infection   sexual contact   in food / water

c) List three typical **symptoms** of active tuberculosis.

1. ....

2. ....

3. ....

Q2 Circle the correct words to complete the following sentences about TB.

a) Some people are infected with the bacteria but don't develop the disease immediately because their immune system / lungs protect(s) them.

b) The bacteria can lie dormant in the body, sometimes for many minutes / years, until the immune system is weakened / strengthened.

c) TB can be prevented by having a vaccination / taking drugs.

d) TB sufferers can be treated with antivirals / antibiotics — they have to take a combination of different ones for a few months.

Q3 **Multi-drug resistant TB** is becoming more common. The graph to the right shows the **development costs** for four new antibiotics that have been developed to treat TB.

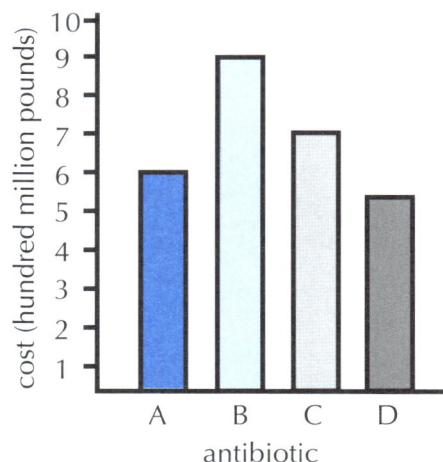

a) Which antibiotic was the **least expensive** to develop?

....

b) Approximately how much did antibiotic **B** cost to develop?

....

c) The high cost of developing new drugs is one reason why so few new drugs emerge. Give **two** reasons **why** it costs a lot of money to develop new drugs.

1. ....

2. ....

Drugs

Q1   Some drugs are **addictive** and can cause **withdrawal symptoms**.

   a)   What are 'withdrawal symptoms'?

      ....

      ....

   b)   Name two drugs that can be addictive.

      ....

Q2   Some drugs can be put into **different groups** according to the effect they have on the **nervous system**.

   a)   Tick the boxes to show whether each drug is a **stimulant** or a **sedative**.

                                    Sedative Stimulant

      i)   Alcohol   ☐   ☐

      ii) Nicotine   ☐   ☐

      iii) Caffeine   ☐   ☐

      iv) Barbiturates   ☐   ☐

   b)   Circle the correct word in each pair to complete the sentences below.

> Sedatives **increase** / **decrease** the activity of the brain. This **slows down** / **speeds up** the responses of the nervous system.
>
> Stimulants **increase** / **decrease** the activity of the brain. This makes you feel **more** / **less** alert and awake.

   c)   Explain why it is **dangerous** to drive or operate machinery when under the influence of a **sedative**.

      ....

      ....

   d)   **Caffeine** is a legal drug in the UK. Why isn't it dangerous to drive under the influence of this drug?

      ....

      ....

Q3   Drugs can **alter behaviour**, leading to poor decisions. Explain how drinking alcohol can increase the risk of **viral infections**.

      ....

      ....

Drugs — Use and Harm

Q1 Look at the following examples of **health problems** and
underline any that you think are related to **smoking tobacco**.

strokes   liver disease   bronchitis   heart attacks   athlete's foot   emphysema

Q2 Smoking tobacco can cause many different **health problems**, including cancer.
However, the habit is still widespread, mainly because smokers find it **difficult to stop**.

a) Explain why people find it difficult to **stop** smoking.

....

b) **Pregnant women** are strongly advised not to smoke.

i) How does smoking whilst pregnant affect the baby's birth weight? Circle the correct answer.

| It's likely to be underweight | | It's likely to be normal weight | | It's likely to be overweight |

ii) Explain how smoking whilst pregnant can cause this problem.

....

....

....

Tobacco smoke contains carbon monoxide.

Q3 The graph shows how the number of
smokers aged between 35 and 54 in
the UK has changed since 1950.

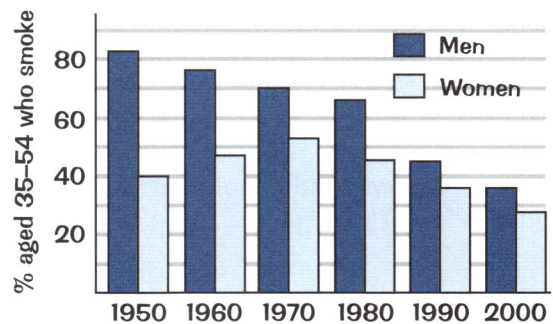

a) Circle the correct word in each pair to
show the main trends in the graph.

i) The number of male smokers has been
increasing / **decreasing** since 1950.

ii) The number of female smokers rose between 1950
and **1970** / **1980**, but then it also began to decrease.

iii) The number of male smokers has been consistently **higher** / **lower**
than the number of female smokers.

b) Why are smokers more likely to suffer from:

i) chest infections? ....

....

....

ii) cancers? ....

....

44

Drugs — Use and Harm

Q4 In the UK, the legal limit for alcohol in the blood when driving is **80 mg per 100 cm³**. The table shows the number of 'units' of alcohol in different drinks. One **unit** increases the blood alcohol level by over **20 mg per 100 cm³** in most people.

DRINK	ALCOHOL UNITS
1 pint of strong lager	3
1 pint of beer	2
1 single measure of whisky	1

a) Bill drinks **two** pints of strong lager. How many units of alcohol has he had? ....

b) **i)** What is Bill's approximate **blood alcohol level**?

....

Assume he drank the pints fairly quickly.

ii) Can Bill **legally** drive in the UK with this blood alcohol level? ....

c) Explain why it can be **dangerous** to drive a car after drinking alcohol.

....

d) Which **organ** is often damaged by excessive alcohol intake? ....

Q5 **Solvents** are useful substances that are sometimes **misused**.

a) Give **three** examples of useful substances that contain potentially dangerous solvents.

....

b) Use some of the words in the box to fill in the gaps and complete the passage.

| decreasing | brain damage | eyes | memory |
| stimulants | breathing | depressants | lungs |

Solvents, like alcohol, are in a group of drugs called ....
Drugs like these affect the nervous system by .... the speed at
which nerve impulses are passed along neurones. Long-term solvent abuse often
causes .... — symptoms of which include personality changes,
trouble sleeping or loss of .... Solvents also damage the
.... and can cause .... difficulties. Solvents can
even kill, and this can happen the very first time you use them.

<u>Painkillers</u>

Q1 **Cannabis** is an **illegal** drug, but some people still use it to relieve the pain caused by **chronic diseases**.

Remember, 'chronic' means long-lasting, not just really bad.

   a) What are cannabinoids?

....

   b) For which diseases is there anecdotal evidence in favour of cannabis as a useful painkiller? Circle the correct answer(s).

chickenpox   arthritis

multiple sclerosis   tuberculosis   food poisoning

Q2 The benefits of some drugs, such as the painkilling chemicals found in **cannabis**, have not been investigated very thoroughly — evidence of the benefits is mainly **anecdotal**.

   a) Why has there been so little research into the medical uses of cannabis compounds? Underline the correct answer(s).

       No scientists were interested in the drug.

       It has been illegal to grow, supply or use cannabis for many years, even for clinical trials.

       Many people believe the dangers of the drug outweigh the benefits.

   b) One breakthrough in the 1980s seemed to support the anecdotal evidence. Explain what this was.

....

....

Q3 **Opiates** are a group of drugs which all have **pain-relieving properties**.

   a) Which of the following drugs are opiates? Tick the boxes next to the correct answers.

     ☐ cannabinoids   ☐ opium

     ☐ ibuprofen   ☐ morphine

     ☐ paracetamol   ☐ aspirin

     ☐ codeine   ☐ amphetamines

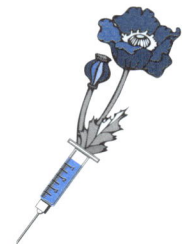

   b) What are all of the opiate drugs derived from?

....

Top Tips: Opium's been used for thousands of years, and it turns out that some of the most famous authors of all time used it. Huxley, Coleridge, Crabbe... Some of them used it really regularly too. Although trying it in your English exams would definitely be a pretty bad move...

Painkillers

Q4   Complete the following passage. You can use each word once, more than once or not at all.

inhibiting	opiates	paracetamol	sensitise	prostaglandins
cannabinoids	transmit	swelling	interfering	ibuprofen

Prostaglandins are chemicals which cause ...., and

.... nerve endings that register pain. Taking drugs like aspirin and

.... relieve pain by .... the formation of

.... Some scientists think that .... might work

in the same way, but others think it acts directly on the brain to stop pain registering.

.... (e.g. morphine and codine) are another type of painkiller —

they work by .... with the way pain-sensing nerve cells

.... messages.

Q5   **Paracetamol** is an over-the-counter drug — you
don't need a prescription from a doctor to obtain it.

a)   Name two specific **symptoms** that are relieved by paracetamol.

....

b)   Suggest **two** reasons why is it important to always read the label
before taking even over-the-counter drugs like paracetamol.

1. ....

2. ....

c)   Paracetamol is a fairly safe drug, but can be very dangerous if too much is taken at once.
Tick the reason(s) that explain this.

☐ Because overdoses of paracetamol can cause terrible liver damage.

☐ Because only a relatively small amount needs to be taken before it is dangerous.

☐ Because paracetamol reduces pain.

☐ Because the damage might not be apparent for several
days after the overdose, by which time it is too late to
stop the person dying from liver failure.

B1b Topic 4 — Use, Misuse and Abuse

Mixed Questions — B1b Topics 3 & 4

Q1   A **reflex action** is an **automatic response** to a stimulus.

a)   Give one advantage of reflex actions to the body.

....

b)   Below are three situations which would cause reflex actions.

   A: Stepping on a drawing pin with bare feet.   **B:** A bright light shining in the eyes.

                              C: Smelling food when hungry.   *Saliva production often increases when you smell food.*

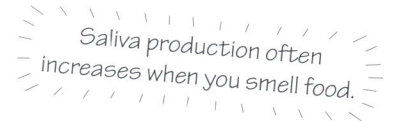

   Complete the table below for each of the examples given above.

	A	B	C
stimulus	pressure of the pin		chemicals in the food
receptor		light receptors	
effector			salivary glands
response		pupil contracts	

c)   Focusing the eye is another reflex action.
   Number the following sentences to show the order of events.

   ☐ The lens becomes thin and the object appears focused.   ☐ The suspensory ligaments pull tight.

   ☐ A message is sent to the CNS along a sensory neurone.   ☐ The ciliary muscles relax.

   ☐ The brain detects the image as unfocused.   ☐ A message is sent to the ciliary muscles.

   ☐ Light receptors detect a distant object.

Q2   **Hormones** are **chemical messengers** that affect particular target cells in the body.

a)   Choose the hormone(s) from the list in blue to go with each of the statements below.

   FSH   **oestrogen**   **insulin**   **progesterone**

   i)   Involved in the menstrual cycle. ....

   ii)   Produced in the pancreas. ....

   iii) Stimulates the ovaries to produce oestrogen. ....

   iv)   Contained in the combined contraceptive pill. ....

b)   Circle the correct words to complete the passage.

   Hormones are released into the **blood / air** and are carried all over the body.

   They affect **all cells / only cells with the right receptors**.

   Hormones **can / cannot** act on different parts of the body at the same time.

c)   When diabetics inject insulin, does their blood sugar level **increase** or **decrease**? ....

Mixed Questions — B1b Topics 3 & 4

Q3 Tuberculosis (TB) is a chronic lung disease caused by a bacterium.

a) Circle the correct word from each pair to complete the sentences below.

The microorganism that causes TB is transmitted by droplet infection / a vector.
This is an example of vertical / horizontal transmission.

b) Explain how the body's defence systems would try to prevent the TB bacterium entering the lungs.

....

c) Name the vaccine that can be used to help prevent TB. ....

d) Why must a combination of antibiotics be taken to treat TB?

....

Q4 The blood is a huge transport system.

a) i) Give the name of the blood cell shown on the right.

....

ii) What is the function of this cell?

....

b) The cell on the right transports oxygen to all parts of the body.

Briefly explain how each of the following adaptations allows
it to do its job well.

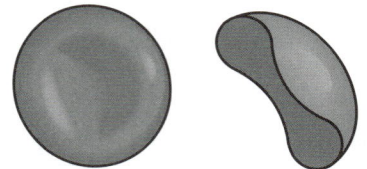

i) Bioconcave disc shape ....

....

ii) Lack of nucleus ....

c) Microorganisms such as HIV can pass from a mother's blood to her child's through the placenta.

Is this horizontal or vertical transmission? ....

Q5 Michael wakes up the morning after his birthday party. He has a terrible headache.
Michael's symptoms were caused by drinking too much alcohol at his party.

a) Is alcohol a **stimulant** or a **sedative**? ....

b) Michael decides to take double the normal dose of paracetamol to ease the pain of his headache.
Tick the boxes that describe why this is **not** a good idea.

☐ You should never exceed the recommended dose of a drug.

☐ Taking too high a dose of paracetamol decreases its effect.

☐ Paracetamol can damage the liver if you take too much.

☐ Paracetamol is particularly dangerous after alcohol.

Atoms

Q1   Substances are made up of **atoms**.

Label this diagram of an atom.

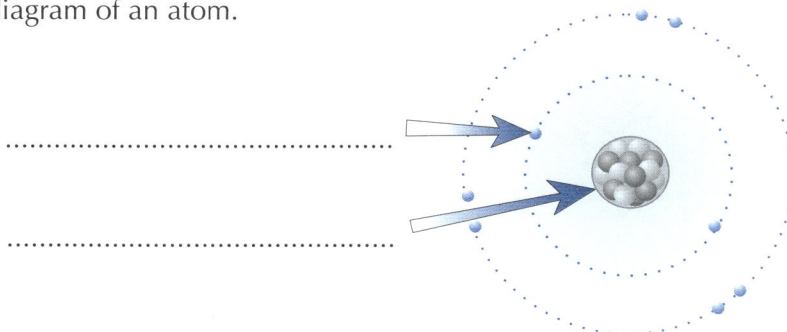

....

....

Q2   Tick the boxes to show whether each sentence is **true** or **false**.

		True	False
a)	Electrons are positively charged.	☐	☐
b)	The nucleus contains protons and electrons.	☐	☐
c)	Electrons have very little mass.	☐	☐
d)	The nucleus has a positive charge.	☐	☐
e)	Electrons are tiny.	☐	☐

Q3   Complete the following sentences by choosing the correct word from each pair.

a)   Neutral atoms have a charge of **0** / **1**.

b)   A neutral atom has the same number of **neutrons** / **protons** and **electrons** / **neutrons**.

c)   If an electron is added to a neutral atom, the atom becomes **positively** / **negatively** charged.

d)   A charged atom is called an **ion** / **isotope**.

Q4   **Complete** this table.

Particle	Mass	Charge
	1	+1
Neutron	1	
Electron		−1

Elements

Q1 Fill in the blanks using the words below to complete the passage about **elements** and **atoms**.

atom   **protons**   **atomic**   **mass**

An element is a substance that is made up from only one type of ....

Atoms of different elements always contain different numbers of ....

and different numbers of electrons. The number of protons in an atom is called the

.... number. The total number of protons and neutrons in an atom is

called the .... number.

Q2 The diagrams below show four different substances. Circle those that contain only **one element**.

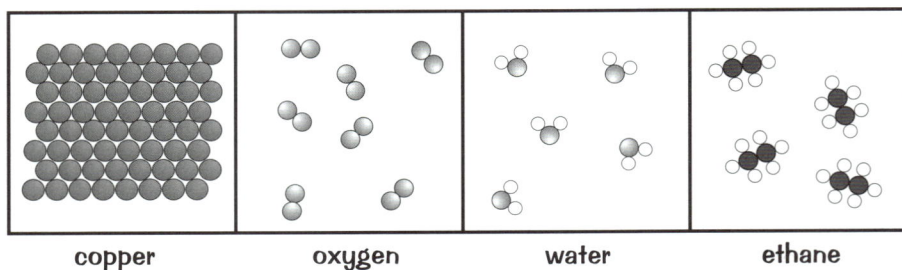

| copper | oxygen | water | ethane |

Q3 This question is about an atom of **magnesium**.

An atom of magnesium can be represented by the following symbol: ⟹ $^{24}_{12}\text{Mg}$

a) What is the **mass number** for this atom? ....

b) What is the **atomic number** for magnesium? ....

c) How many neutrons does this atom of magnesium contain? ....

Q4 Many everyday substances, e.g. gold and aluminium, are **elements**.
Other substances, like air and sugar, are not.

Explain what this means in terms of the **atoms** in these substances.

....

....

Mixtures and Compounds

Q1   Correctly label the following diagrams with 'element', 'mixture' or 'compound'.

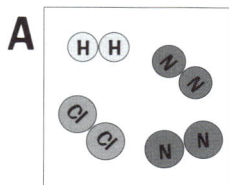

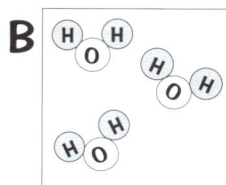

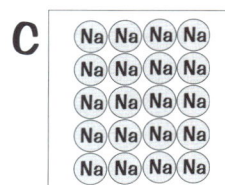

A
B
C

a) ....   b) ....   c) ....

Q2   Circle the correct words to complete the following paragraphs.

> Compounds / Atoms are formed when two or more elements chemically join
>
> together. The chemicals produced are usually very difficult to separate / join
>
> back into elements using physical methods.
>
> The properties of compounds are identical to / different from those of the
>
> elements used to make them.
>
> Mixtures are usually relatively easy to separate / join because there are no
>
> chemical bonds / atoms between their different parts.

Q3   Circle the correct answer for each of the following questions.

a)   Which elements are present in potassium bromide?

potassium and bromine   potassium and bromide   potassium, bromine and water

b)   What compound is produced when calcium and chlorine react?

calcium chlorine   calcium chloride   calcium dichloride

Q4   The **formula** of copper(II) carbonate is $CuCO_3$.

a)   How many **atoms** of **carbon** are shown in this formula?

....

b)   Is copper(II) carbonate a **compound**, an **element** or a **mixture**?

....

c)   In total, how many **atoms** are shown in the **formula**?

....

Mixtures and Compounds

Q5 Complete the table by putting the substances in the correct columns.

sugar   carbon monoxide   copper   sulphur   salt

air   gold   carbon dioxide   milk

elements	compounds	mixtures

Q6 The diagram shows some of the **atoms** in air.

a) In total, how many atoms are shown in the diagram?

....

b) What is the formula of the compound shown in the diagram?

....

c) Explain why the nitrogen in the diagram is not a compound.

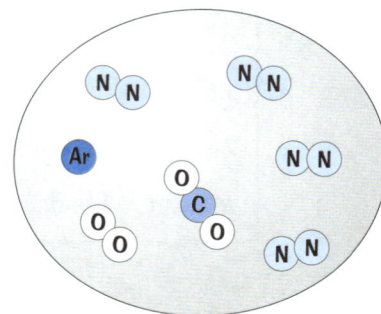

....

Q7 Hassan mixes some **iron** filings and some yellow **sulphur** powder together in a beaker and leaves them overnight. The next day he holds a magnet over the beaker and the iron filings jump up and stick to it.

a) Did the iron and sulphur react to form a compound when they were left together? How can you tell?

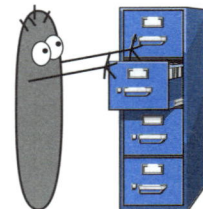

....

....

b) Hassan tries heating the mixture. This causes the yellowy mixture to turn grey. Which of the following statements best describes why the yellow colour disappears? Underline your answer.

A The sulphur has evaporated.   B The sulphur has reacted with the iron.
C Sulphur changes colour when heated.   D The iron has expanded and is hiding the sulphur.

Top Tips: It's really important that you know the difference between mixtures and compounds. Take some time to learn it properly, and you'll pick up some easy marks in the exam.

C1a Topic 5 — Patterns in Properties

Chemical Reactions

Q1 Below is a list of three chemical reactions. For each one write next to it how quick the reaction is — **fast**, **medium** or **slow**.

    A   A steel hinge rusting ....

    B   A firework exploding ....

    C   A piece of aluminium reacting with an acid ....

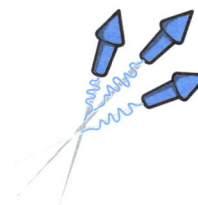

Q2 This **equation** shows the formation of **carbon dioxide** when carbon is burned in air:

$$C + O_2 \rightarrow CO_2$$

a) Name the **reactants** in this equation.

....

b) Name the **product** in this equation.

....

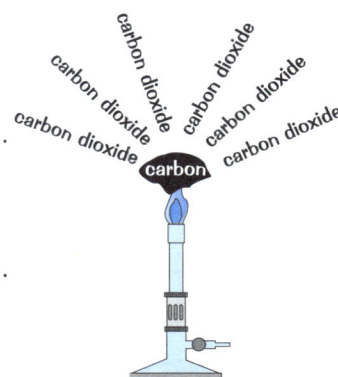

Q3 Circle the correct words to complete the following paragraphs.

a) Exothermic reactions **take in** / **give out** energy, usually in the form of **heat** / **sound**. This is often shown by a **fall** / **rise** in **temperature** / **mass**.

b) Endothermic reactions **take in** / **give out** energy, usually in the form of **heat** / **sound**. This is often shown by a **fall** / **rise** in **temperature** / **mass**.

Q4 List all the reactants and products in each of the following reactions.

a) When magnesium burns in air it reacts with the oxygen present to form a white smoke of magnesium oxide.

Reactants: ....   Products: ....

b) If magnesium carbonate is heated it decomposes to form magnesium oxide and carbon dioxide.

Reactants: ....   Products: ....

c) A piece of potassium metal will react with water to produce potassium hydroxide and hydrogen gas.

Reactants: ....   Products: ....

Chemical Reactions

Q5 Limestone (**calcium carbonate**) decomposes when it's heated, to form quicklime (**calcium oxide**) and **carbon dioxide**.

a) Write the word equation for this reaction.

....

b) The reaction requires a large amount of heat. Is it **exothermic** or **endothermic**?
Explain your answer.

....

Q6 Examples of exothermic reactions are **burning fuels** and **neutralisation reactions**.

In this list of reactions, write **B** for burning fuel or **N** for neutralisation reaction next to each one.

☐ sulphuric acid + sodium hydroxide → sodium sulphate + water

☐ methane + oxygen → carbon dioxide + water

☐ potassium hydroxide + hydrochloric acid → potassium chloride + water

☐ ethanol + oxygen → carbon dioxide + water

Q7 In an experiment to investigate **reaction rates**, strips of **magnesium** were put into tubes containing different concentrations of **hydrochloric acid**. The time taken for the magnesium to 'disappear' was measured. The results are shown in the table.

Conc. of acid (mol/dm^3)	Time taken (s)
0.01	298
0.02	147
0.04	74
0.08	37
0.10	30
0.20	15

a) Give two things that should be kept the same in each case to make this a fair test.

....

....

b) Plot a graph of the data on the grid provided, with the concentration of the acid on the horizontal axis and the time on the vertical axis.

c) What do the results tell you about how the concentration affects the rate of the reaction?

....

A Brief History of the Periodic Table

Q1 Fill in the gaps using the words provided to complete the following passage.

properties   atomic mass   periodic   reactive

Early versions of the periodic table listed the known elements in

order of their .... When this was done it was

found that .... of the elements, such as how

.... they were, repeated at regular intervals.

These are known as .... patterns.

carbon, nitrogen, oxygen, fluorine

Q2 Circle the correct words to complete the sentences.

a) Mendeleev left gaps in his table for undiscovered **elements** / **compounds**.

b) Mendeleev arranged the elements in order of **decreasing** / **increasing** atomic number.

c) Mendeleev was able to predict the **names** / **properties** of undiscovered elements.

d) Elements with similar properties appeared in the same **columns** / **rows**.

Q3 Mendeleev predicted the discovery of an element that would fill a gap in his Group 4, and he called it '**ekasilicon**'.

The table shows the **densities** of known elements in this group.

'Ekasilicon' was eventually discovered and given another name. Use the table to decide which of the elements below is ekasilicon. Circle your choice.

Element	Density g/cm³
carbon	2.27
silicon	2.33
ekasilicon	
tin	7.31
lead	11.3

palladium, 12.0 g/cm³

germanium, 5.32 g/cm³

beryllium, 1.85 g/cm³

copper, 8.96 g/cm³

Look for a pattern in the densities of the elements.

Q4 Tick the boxes to show whether the following statements are **true** or **false**.

	True	False

a) New elements have been found which fit into the gaps left in Mendeleev's table. ☐ ☐

b) The noble gases were included in the early forms of the periodic table. ☐ ☐

c) Neon was missing from Mendeleev's table as it hadn't been discovered yet. ☐ ☐

The Periodic Table

Q1 Name the different parts of the periodic table using the following labels.

reactive metals   noble gases   poor metals   transition metals   non-metals

a) ....

b) ....

c) ....

d) ....

e) ....

	Group 1	Group 2											Group 3	Group 4	Group 5	Group 6	Group 7	Group 0
					H													He
2	Li	Be											B	C	N	O	F	Ne
3	Na	Mg											Al	Si	P	S	Cl	Ar
4	K	Ca	Sc	Ti	V	Cr	Mn	Fe	Co	Ni	Cu	Zn	Ga	Ge	As	Se	Br	Kr
5	Rb	Sr	Y	Zr	Nb	Mo	Tc	Ru	Rh	Pd	Ag	Cd	In	Sn	Sb	Te	I	Xe
6	Cs	Ba	57-71 Lanthanides	Hf	Ta	W	Re	Os	Ir	Pt	Au	Hg	Tl	Pb	Bi	Po	At	Rn
7	Fr	Ra	89-103 Actinides															

Q2 Decide whether the following statements are **true** or **false**.

	True	False
a) Elements in the same group have the same number of electrons in their outer shells.	☐	☐
b) The periodic table shows the elements in order of descending atomic number.	☐	☐
c) Each horizontal row in the periodic table contains elements with similar properties.	☐	☐
d) The periodic table includes all the known compounds.	☐	☐
e) A period in the periodic table is a horizontal row of elements.	☐	☐
f) Elements in the same group have similar properties.	☐	☐

Q3 **Argon** is an extremely unreactive gas. Use the periodic table to name two more elements that you would expect to have **similar properties** to argon.

....

Q4 Use a periodic table to help you answer the following questions.

a) Name one element in the same period as silicon.   ....

b) Name one element in the same group as potassium.   ....

c) Name one element that is a halogen.   ....

d) Name one element that is an alkali metal.   ....

Group 1 — The Alkali Metals

Q1   Highlight the location of the alkali metals on this periodic table.

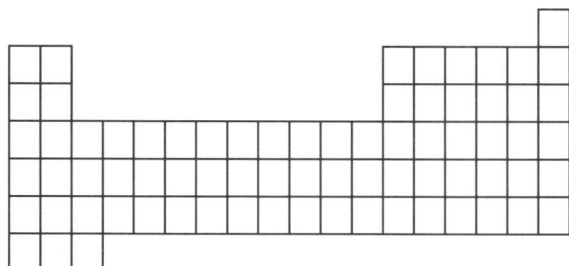

Q2   **Sodium**, **potassium** and **lithium** are all alkali metals.

a)   Put sodium, potassium and lithium in order of increasing reactivity.

least reactive   ....

....

most reactive   ....

b)   Explain why alkali metals all have similar properties.

....

Q3   Tick the correct boxes to show whether the statements below are **true** or **false**.

True   False

a)   Alkali metals are very reactive.

b)   Calcium is an alkali metal.

c)   Alkali metals are stored in oil to stop them reacting with oxygen and water in the air.

d)   Alkali metal atoms all have a single electron in their outer shell.

Q4   Circle the correct words to complete the passage below.

Potassium is a soft metal with **one** / **two** electron(s) in its outer shell. It reacts vigorously with water, producing **potassium dioxide** / **potassium hydroxide** and **hydrogen** / **oxygen** gas. When it reacts, it loses its outermost **proton** / **electron**, forming an ion with a **positive** / **negative** charge.

Top Tips: Make sure that when it comes to your exam, you're all clued up on the alkali metals. You need to know where they are in the periodic table, and what goes on in their reactions with water. Make sure you know about how their reactivity changes as you go down the group too.

Group 1 — The Alkali Metals

Q5 Martin dropped equal-sized pieces of three different **alkali metals**, A, B and C, into bowls of water and timed how long it took for each piece to **vanish**. His results are shown in the table.

METAL	TIME TAKEN TO VANISH (s)
A	27
B	8
C	42

a) **i)** Which is the most reactive metal? ....

ii) How can you tell?

....

b) The three metals used were lithium, sodium and potassium. Use the results shown in the table to match them up to the correct letters A, B and C.

A = ...

B = ...

C = ...

c) Martin noticed that a particular gas was always produced in these reactions. Which gas is this?

....

d) Suggest how Martin may have identified the gas produced.

....

....

Q6 Archibald put a piece of **sodium** into a beaker of water.

a) Write a word equation for the reaction that occurs between sodium and water.

....

b) After the reaction had finished, Archibald tested the liquid in the beaker with universal indicator. What colour change would he see and why?

....

....

c) Would the following alkali metals react **more** or **less** vigorously than sodium with water? Explain your answers.

Think about how close the outer electron is to the nucleus.

i) lithium ....

....

ii) potassium ....

....

Group 7 — The Halogens

Q1 Highlight the location of the halogens in this periodic table.

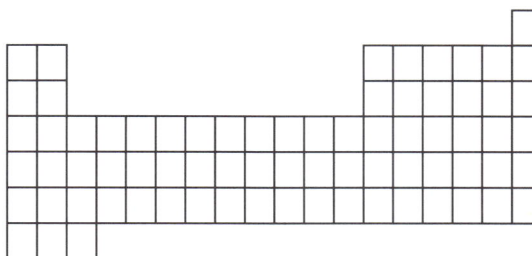

Q2 Draw lines to match the halogens to their **descriptions**.

bromine

chlorine

fluorine

iodine

green gas

grey solid

red-brown liquid

yellow gas

Q3 Chlorine, bromine, fluorine and iodine are all **halogens**.

a) Put these four halogens in order of **increasing** reactivity.

least reactive ....

....

....

most reactive ....

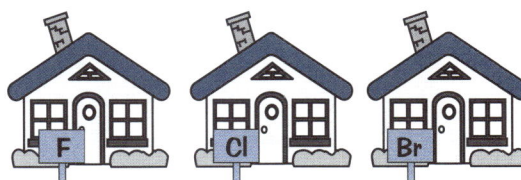

F   Cl   Br

b) Why do all the halogens have similar properties?

....

Q4 Tick the boxes to show whether the statements are **true** or **false**.

		True	False
a)	Iodine is more reactive than chlorine.	☐	☐
b)	The atomic number increases down the group.	☐	☐
c)	The halogens become darker in colour as you move down the group.	☐	☐
d)	Chlorine is used in bleach and swimming pools to kill bacteria.	☐	☐
e)	Iodine is used as a flavouring.	☐	☐
f)	Their boiling points increase going down the group.	☐	☐

Group 7 — The Halogens

Q5   Fill in the blanks in the following equations.

a)   .... + bromine → aluminium bromide

b)   Potassium + ... → potassium iodide

c)   Magnesium + fluorine → ....

Q6   **Sodium** was reacted with **bromine vapour** using the equipment shown.
White crystals of a new solid were formed during the reaction.

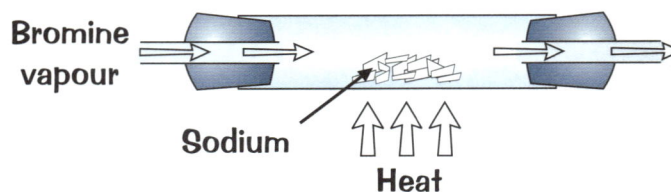

Bromine vapour

Sodium

Heat

a)   Name the white crystals.

....

b)   Write a word equation for the reaction.

....

Q7   Equal volumes of **bromine water** were added to three test tubes, each containing a different **halogen salt solution**. The results are shown in the table.

SOLUTION	RESULT
potassium chloride	no reaction
potassium iodide	reaction

a)   Explain why there was no reaction when bromine water was added to potassium chloride solution.

....

....

b) i)   Explain why there was a reaction with the potassium iodide solution.

....

....

ii) Write a word equation for the reaction in the potassium iodide solution.

....

c)   What is this type of reaction known as?

....

Group 0 — The Noble Gases

Q1 Circle the correct word(s) in each pair to complete the following sentences about **noble gases**.

a) The elements of Group 0 are all brightly coloured / colourless gases.

b) Group 0 elements are inert / reactive.

c) All Group 0 elements need to gain / lose / neither gain nor lose electrons to fill their outer shells.

Q2 Complete the passage about noble gases by choosing from the words below.

balloons	red	light bulbs	reactive	lower	blue
shop signs	airships	higher	inert	telephones	green

Neon is used in .... as it gives out a bright

.... light. Helium is used in ....

and .... as it has a .... density than

air. Argon is used in .... — the ....

atmosphere stops the hot filament from burning away.

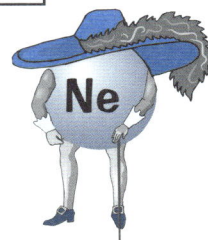

Q3 The noble gases were **discovered** long after many of the other elements.

a) Why did it take scientists so long to discover the noble gases?

....

....

b) Explain why the noble gases are unreactive.

....

....

c) What can be done to noble gases to make them visible?

....

Top Tips: The examiners will expect you to know quite a bit about certain **groups** in the periodic table — the **halogens**, the **alkali metals**, the **noble gases** and the **transition metals**. Make sure you're clear on their general properties and how these change as you move down or up each group.

Metals and Their Uses

Q1 Most **metals** that are used to make everyday objects are found in the **central section** of the periodic table.

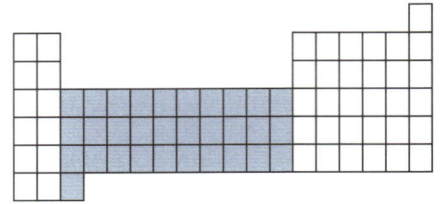

a) What name is given to this group of metals?

....

b) Many of the metals in this group form colourful compounds. Give two uses of this property.

....

Q2 Which of the following statements are **true** and which are **false**?

True False

a) All metals are good conductors of heat.

b) In the periodic table, metals are on the far right-hand side.

c) Most metals have a high density.

d) Most metals can be bent and are strong.

e) Only a few metals conduct electricity.

Q3 What **properties** would you look for if you were asked to choose a **metal** suitable for making knives and forks?

....

....

....

Q4 Match up the names of the following **metals** to their **properties** and **uses**.

a) **Gold**

b) **Copper**

c) **Iron**

| Malleable |
| Shiny |
| Conducts electricity very well |

Electrical wiring

Jewellery

Gates and railings

C1a Topic 5 — Patterns in Properties

Metals and Their Uses

Q5 Imagine that a space probe has brought a sample of a new element back from Mars. Scientists think that the element is a **metal**, but they aren't certain. Give **three properties** they could look for to provide evidence that the element is a **metal**.

1. ....

2. ....

3. ....

Q6 For each of the following **applications** of metals, say which **property** of the metal makes it ideal for the given use. Choose the best answer from the list of typical properties of metals below. You may only use each property **once**.

ductile   **malleable**   **resists corrosion**   **conducts heat**

a) Iron bars are hammered into shape to make horseshoes. ....

b) Copper is used to make the bases of saucepans and frying pans. ....

c) Gold is used by dentists to make long-lasting fillings and false teeth. ....

d) Copper is drawn out into thin wires for electrical cables. ....

Q7 This table shows some of the **properties** of four different **metals**.

Metal	Heat conduction	Cost	Resistance to corrosion	Strength
1	average	high	excellent	good
2	average	medium	good	excellent
3	excellent	low	good	good
4	low	high	average	poor

Use the information in the table to choose which metal would be **best** for making each of the following, and explain your choice.

a) Saucepan bases ....

....

b) Car bodies ....

....

c) A statue to be placed in a town centre ....

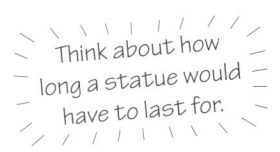
Think about how long a statue would have to last for.

....

Identifying Compounds

Q1   Put these stages in order to describe the method of a **flame test**.

☐ Dip a wire loop into a powdered sample of the compound to be tested.

☐ Record what colour flame is produced.

☐ Place the end of the wire loop into a blue Bunsen flame.

☐ Dip a wire loop into some hydrochloric acid.

Q2   Match up the metals with the colour of the flame that they produce.

calcium   lilac

potassium   blue-green

copper   yellow/orange

sodium   brick-red

Q3   Complete the following passage about precipitation tests using the words below.

chemical reaction   precipitate   sodium hydroxide

metal   potassium hydroxide   colour

You can use each word more than once.

You can sometimes find out what .... an unknown

substance contains by adding it in solution to .... solution.

A .... occurs and a .... containing

the metal is formed. This compound has a characteristic ....

depending on the .... it contains.

Q4   Three **metal compounds**, X, Y and Z, are tested to try and find out which metal they contain. The results of the tests are shown in the table.

Compound	Colour of Precipitate formed with NaOH
X	Blue
Y	White
Z	Sludgy red

Identify the compound that contains these metals:

Zinc = ...   **Iron** = ...   **Copper** = ...

C1a Topic 5 — Patterns in Properties

Identifying Compounds

Q5 James has a sample of a substance that he thinks might be table salt, which is the compound **sodium chloride**.

a) What could James do to provide evidence that the substance contains sodium?

....

....

....

b) **i)** If his test gave him the result that he expected, does this prove that the substance is table salt?

....

ii) Would it be safe to put this onto food if his test was positive? Explain your answer.

....

....

Q6 Burglar Bill broke into Dr Atom's chemistry lab and took a jar containing a mystery substance. Burglar Bill was traced by the chemistry police and Dr Atom was asked to identify the substance.

Dr Atom placed some of the substance in water. A vigorous reaction took place and the substance burnt with a lilac flame. Dr Atom was able to identify the substance from this test.

a) What could the jar have contained?

....

b) What group in the periodic table does this substance belong to?

....

c) What test could Dr Atom have done to confirm his identification of the substance?

....

....

Top Tips: In your exam, you'll need to show that you'd know how to identify an unknown substance — by coming up with a suitable experiment. You might also be given the results of an experiment and have to identify substances from the data. It's a bit like being a detective...

C1a Topic 6 — Making Changes

Chemicals in Food

Q1   Indicate whether the substances below occur **naturally** or are only made **artificially**.

	Natural	Artificial
a) glucose	☐	☐
b) vanillin (vanilla flavour)	☐	☐
c) saccharin	☐	☐
d) tartrazine (yellow colouring)	☐	☐

Lots of substances that occur naturally can also be made artificially. Don't worry about that — if it's found in nature, just tick 'natural'.

Wow mummy, look at that octyl ethanoate tree

Q2   Match up the boxes to complete the sentences.

A natural substance...

An artificial substance...

Cooking food...

...produces new substances.

...is a chemical that exists in nature.

...is a chemical that's manufactured by people.

Q3   Natural vanilla contains the chemical **vanillin**.
Vanillin is also made artificially for use in ice cream.

a)   What is responsible for the difference in flavour between natural vanilla and that in ice cream?

....

....

b)   Is naturally occurring vanillin **chemically different** from artificially made vanillin?

....

c)   Some artificial flavours, e.g. artificial sweeteners, have a similar flavour to natural substances but a different chemical structure.

   i)   Give an example of an artificial sweetener with a different structure from sugar.

....

   ii)   Explain why this difference in chemical structure is an advantage.

....

....

Chemicals in Food

Q4 Tick the correct boxes to show whether the following statements are **true** or **false**.

	True	False
a) Cooking is a reversible chemical change.	☐	☐
b) Some artificial food additives have been linked to health problems.	☐	☐
c) Cooked potatoes contain different chemicals from raw potatoes.	☐	☐
d) Aspartame is a natural sweetener.	☐	☐

Q5 Health problems have been linked to both artificial and natural additives.

Give an example of a health problem associated with each type of additive.

a) artificial ....

b) natural ....

Q6 Read the following passage and answer the questions below.

> Cooking causes irreversible changes and produces new substances. For example, eggs and meat contain protein molecules. The energy from cooking breaks some of the chemical bonds in the protein molecules and gives the food a more edible texture. Raw potato is indigestible for humans because potato cells have a cellulose wall which we can't break down. The cooking process breaks down the cellulose cell wall, making the potato easily digestible.

a) Give two examples of chemical changes caused by cooking.

....

....

b) Do fried eggs contain all the same chemicals as raw eggs? Explain your answer.

....

....

Top Tips: The important thing to remember here is that there's nothing special about 'natural' compounds — they can all be copied if you can manage to stick the right atoms together in the right way.

Acids and Bases and Neutralisation

Q1 Complete the following sentences by circling the correct word.

a) Solutions which are not acidic or alkaline are said to be natural / neutral.

b) When a substance is neutral it has a pH of 0 / 7.

c) Indigestion occurs because the stomach produces too much hydrochloric / sulphuric acid.

d) Ammonia is used to make additives / fertilisers like ammonium nitrate.

Q2 Draw lines to match the substances below to their **universal indicator colour**, **pH value** and **acid/base strength**.

SUBSTANCE	UNIVERSAL INDICATOR COLOUR	PH	ACID/BASE STRENGTH
a) distilled water	purple	5/6	strong alkali
b) rainwater	yellow	8/9	weak alkali
c) caustic soda	dark green/blue	14	weak acid
d) washing-up liquid	red	7	neutral
e) car battery acid	pale green	1	strong acid

Q3 The table shows the **pH** of a range of substances.

a) Which substance from the table is:

i) the weakest acid? ....

ii) the weakest alkali? ....

iii) the strongest acid? ....

iv) the strongest alkali? ....

v) neutral? ....

SUBSTANCE	pH
car battery acid	1
vinegar	3
lemonade	5
alcohol	7
toothpaste	9
ammonia solution	11
sodium hydroxide solution	13

b) List any two substances from the table that could neutralise each other.

....

c) i) Complete the general equation below for the reaction between an acid and a base.

ACID + BASE → .... + ...

ii) Circle the correct term for this kind of reaction.

decomposition / oxidation / neutralisation

Acids and Bases and Neutralisation

Q4 Acids and bases have many different **uses**. For each of the uses given below, circle the correct acid or base from the pair.

a) Acid used in the production of petrol, nylon and detergents. hydrochloric acid / phosphoric acid

b) Base used to manufacture nitric acid and sodium carbonate. ammonia / sodium hydroxide

c) Acid used as a food additive to give foods a sour taste. citric acid / hydrochloric acid

d) Base used to make bleach and in soap manufacture. ammonia / sodium hydroxide

e) Acid that is diluted and used as a descaling agent. ethanoic acid / hydrochloric acid

f) Acid used to manufacture PVC and to process steel. phosphoric acid / hydrochloric acid

Q5 **Antacid tablets** contain **alkalis** to neutralise the excess stomach acid that causes indigestion.

Joey wanted to test whether some antacid tablets really did neutralise acid. He added a tablet to some hydrochloric acid, stirred it and tested its pH. Further tests were carried out after adding a second, third and fourth tablet. His results are shown in the table below.

TABLETS ADDED	PH OF THE ACID
0	1
1	2
2	3
3	7
4	7

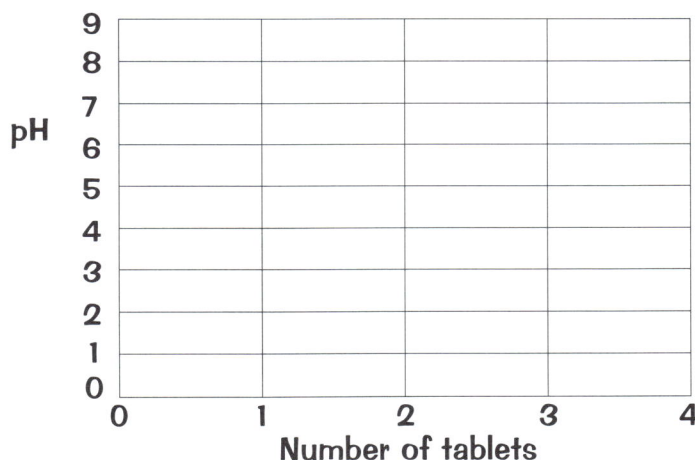

a) i) Plot a graph of the results.

ii) Describe how the pH changes when the tablets are added to the acid.

....

....

iii) How do the results show that the tablets reduce acidity?

....

iv) How many tablets were needed to neutralise the acid?

....

b) Joey tested another brand of tablets, brand X, to see whether they were better at removing acidity. He found that only **two** tablets were required to neutralise the acid.

Make a sketch on the graph of the results you might expect for these tablets and label it 'brand X'.

Think carefully about what would happen to the line after adding the second tablet.

Reactions of Acids

Q1   Give the **general word equation** for the reaction between an **acid** and:

   a)   a **metal carbonate**   ....

   b)   a **metal hydroxide**   ....

   c)   a **metal oxide**   ....

Q2   Complete the word equations for **acids** reacting with **metal oxides**.

   a)   sulphuric acid + zinc oxide → .... + ...

   b)   hydrochloric acid + ... oxide → nickel .... + ...

Q3   Complete the word equations for **acids** reacting with **metal hydroxides**.

   a)   sulphuric acid + calcium hydroxide → .... + ...

   b)   hydrochloric acid + ... hydroxide → nickel .... + ...

Q4   Amir was investigating a way of restoring a tarnished copper ornament. He got three different **copper compounds**, reacted each one with dilute **hydrochloric acid** and wrote down his observations.

SUBSTANCE TESTED	FORMULA	COLOUR	OBSERVATIONS WHEN ADDED TO THE ACID
copper carbonate	$CuCO_3$	green	fizzed and dissolved forming a blue solution
copper hydroxide	$Cu(OH)_2$	blue	dissolved slowly forming a blue solution
copper oxide	CuO	black	dissolved very slowly forming a blue solution

   a)   **i)**   Why does copper carbonate fizz when it reacts with the acid?

Think about what is produced in the reaction.

....

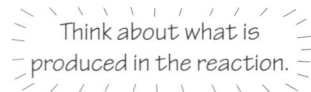

      ii)   Write a word equation for the reaction.

....

   b)   Amir tested part of the copper ornament with the acid and it fizzed.

      i)   Which compound is likely to be present on the surface of the ornament?

....

      ii)   What further evidence would support this?

....

Top Tips: It's really important that you know what's produced in the reactions of acids with metal oxides, hydroxides and carbonates. It'll make writing equations much simpler — thumbs up.

Preparing Salts and Hazard Symbols

Q1 Insoluble salts can be made in precipitation reactions.

Circle the two compounds from each set of options
which could be used to make the given insoluble salt.

a) **copper carbonate**: calcium chloride / sodium carbonate / copper nitrate

b) **calcium sulphate**: calcium chloride / copper nitrate / sodium sulphate

c) **lead sulphate**: sodium carbonate / lead nitrate / sodium sulphate

Q2 Silver chloride is an insoluble salt that can be produced using a precipitation reaction.

a) Which two solutions could be used to make silver chloride? Circle your answers.

barium chloride   potassium nitrate   silver nitrate   barium sulphate

b) Describe how you could produce a pure, dry sample of silver chloride.

....

....

....

Q3 Draw lines to match the **symbols** below with their **meanings** and **hazards**.

a) **toxic** can cause death if swallowed, inhaled or absorbed through the skin

b) **corrosive** causes reddening or blistering of the skin

c) **irritant** attacks and destroys living tissue

Q4 **Potassium chlorate** has this **hazard symbol** on its container:

a) Explain what the symbol means and briefly describe why potassium chlorate is dangerous.

....

b) Potassium chlorate is one of the chemicals used in match heads. Describe its function.

....

c) Explain why potassium chlorate is stored separately from flammable or combustible materials.

....

Hydration and Thermal Decomposition

Q1   Answer the following questions about reactions involving **water**.

   a)   Which reaction(s) involve **dehydration**? Circle one or more letters.

   A   copper hydroxide $\rightarrow$ copper oxide + water

   B   ethene + water $\rightarrow$ ethanol

   C   nickel carbonate $\rightarrow$ nickel oxide + carbon dioxide

   b)   Which reaction(s) involve **hydration**? Circle one or more letters.

   A   hydrated copper sulphate $\rightarrow$ anhydrous copper sulphate + water

   B   calcium oxide + water $\rightarrow$ calcium hydroxide

   C   methane + oxygen $\rightarrow$ carbon dioxide + water

   D   glucose $\rightarrow$ carbon + water

Q2   Indicate whether the following statements are **true** or **false**.

		True	False
a)	Calcium carbonate gives off carbon dioxide and water when it decomposes.	☐	☐
b)	Thermal decomposition involves breaking a substance down into simpler substances.	☐	☐
c)	Baking powder produces carbon dioxide when heated, which makes cakes rise.	☐	☐
d)	Sugar can be hydrated by adding it to concentrated sulphuric acid.	☐	☐
e)	The dehydration of sugar gives carbon and water as its products.	☐	☐

Q3   When **hydrated copper sulphate** (blue crystals) is heated it turns into **anhydrous copper sulphate** (white powder) and **water**.

   hydrated copper sulphate $\rightarrow$ anhydrous copper sulphate + water

   a)   Why is the reaction described as dehydration?

   ....

   b)   Why can the reaction also be described as thermal decomposition?

   ....

   c)   Why is the reverse reaction described as hydration?

   ....

   d)   Explain how the reverse reaction can be used as a simple test for water.

   ....

Hydration and Thermal Decomposition

Q4 Sam wanted to test whether **baking powder** really does **decompose** and give off gas when heated.

She put some baking powder on a tin lid and placed it in an oven at 220 °C.
After 20 minutes there appeared to be no change to the white powder.

a) Why do you think there was no apparent change?

(Assume that some of the baking powder decomposed.)

....

b) Explain fully what she could have done to show that decomposition had occurred.

....

....

c) Baking powder contains sodium hydrogencarbonate.
Write a word equation for the thermal decomposition of sodium hydrogencarbonate.

....

d) Explain what thermal decomposition means.

....

e) Explain how baking soda is able to make a cake rise when it is heated in the oven.

....

....

Q5 Richard used the apparatus shown to try and prove that carbon dioxide was formed when baking soda was heated.

baking soda — tiny liquid drops — liquid A

heat gently

a) **i)** What are the liquid droplets?

....

ii) Why do they form on the part of the test tube shown?

....

b) **i)** Name liquid A and say what it is used for.

....

ii) Describe the change that would occur in liquid A during the reaction.

....

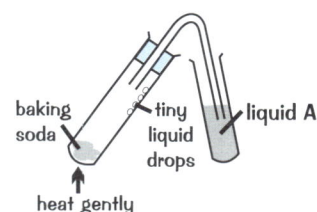

Top Tips: This stuff isn't too tricky if you learn the rules behind it — hydration reactions have water as a reactant and dehydration reactions have water as a product. When it comes to carbonates and hydrogencarbonates, learn the word equations and you can't go far wrong.

Metal Ores

Q1 Answer the following questions using data from the reactivity series shown.

a) Which element is the most reactive?

....

b) Which elements can be extracted from their ores by heating with carbon monoxide?

....

c) Which element would be the easiest to extract from its ore?

....

The Reactivity Series

potassium
sodium
calcium
magnesium
aluminium
CARBON
zinc
iron
tin
lead

Q2 Circle the correct words to complete the passage below.

Carbon / Water can be used to extract metals that are above / below it in the reactivity series. Oxygen is removed from metal oxides in a process called oxidation / reduction. Other metals have to be extracted using electrolysis / dehydration because they are less / more reactive.

Q3 Copper may have first been extracted when someone accidentally dropped some copper ore into a **wood fire**. When the ashes were cleared away some copper was left.

a) Explain how dropping the ore into the fire led to the extraction of copper.

....

b) Why do you think that copper was one of the first metals to be extracted from its ore?

....

Q4 Some metals are found as **ores**. Others, such as gold, are usually found as **elements**.

a) Explain why gold is usually found as an element.

....

b) i) Magnetite, a type of iron ore, is formed from iron and oxygen in the following reaction:

$$3Fe + 2O_2 \rightarrow Fe_3O_4$$

Is the iron **oxidised** or **reduced** in this reaction? ....

ii) Aluminium is extracted from its ore, aluminium oxide, using electrolysis.

$$2Al_2O_3 \rightarrow 4Al + 3O_2$$

Is the aluminium **oxidised** or **reduced** in this reaction? ....

Gas Tests

Q1   Which piece(s) of apparatus shown could be used to collect:

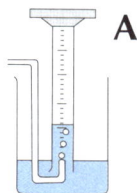

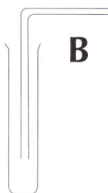

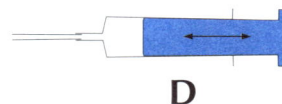

A   B   C   D

a)   a gas by downward delivery?   ....

b)   a sample of dry ammonia gas?   ....

c)   a gas by upward delivery?   ....

d)   a specific volume of carbon dioxide?   ....

e)   a soluble gas and monitor the rate at which it is produced?   ....

Carbon dioxide is only slightly soluble in water.

Q2   A number of **gases** were collected and **tested**. Of the gases listed, which gas:

oxygen	chlorine	carbon dioxide
	hydrogen	ammonia

a)   bleached damp litmus paper?   ....

b)   gave a 'pop' when tested with a burning splint?   ....

c)   turned damp red litmus paper blue?   ....

d)   relit a glowing splint?   ....

Q3   When copper carbonate is heated it gives off **carbon dioxide**.

a)   Complete the diagram to show how you could collect a test tube of the gas by **downward delivery**.

b)   Why is downward delivery a suitable collection method for carbon dioxide?

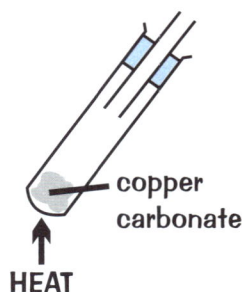

....

....

copper carbonate

HEAT

c)   If potassium chlorate ($KClO_3$) is heated, a gas is produced that can be collected. Jenny thought that chlorine or oxygen might be given off.

How could she test to see which gas is given off?

....

....

Gas Tests

Q4 A flask of **dry ammonia** was collected using the apparatus shown.

a) Explain why ammonia is suitable for collection by upward delivery.

....

b) Damp litmus paper is used to test the gas when the flask is full. What colour litmus paper would be used and what colour change would occur?

....

....

Diagram labels: test with litmus paper; dry ammonia gas; potassium hydroxide pellets; concentrated ammonia solution; HEAT GENTLY

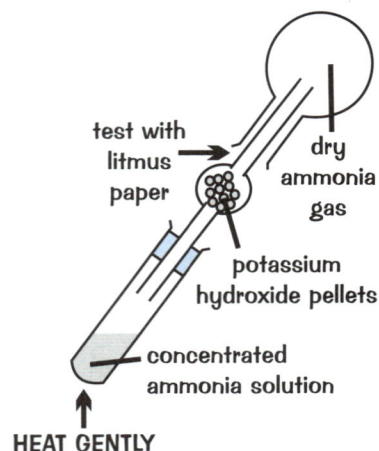

Q5 Jamie wanted to produce a gas jar full of **hydrogen** for an experiment. He knew that **zinc** could be reacted with **sulphuric acid** to produce the gas.

a) Describe how Jamie could collect a full gas jar of hydrogen and draw a labelled diagram of the apparatus he should use, showing how more acid could be added during the reaction.

....

....

....

Think about the density and solubility of hydrogen when planning the apparatus.

b) Write a word equation for the reaction that takes place.

....

c) Explain how Jamie could test the gas produced to make sure that it was hydrogen.

....

Top Tips: Remember, the collection method depends on how dense the gas is. If it's 'lighter than air', upward delivery should be used. If it's 'heavier than air', it's downward delivery you need.

C1a Topic 6 — Making Changes

Mixed Questions — C1a Topics 5 & 6

Q1 This question concerns **substances A to I** below.

A fluorine	**B** sodium chloride	**C** copper sulphate
D nitrogen	**E** carbon dioxide	**F** sulphur
G sodium	**H** graphite	**I** magnesium oxide

a) **i)** Which of the substances A to I are present in air?

....

ii) Explain whether the forces between the molecules in air are strong or weak.

....

b) **i)** Which substance is often used as a natural food additive? ....

ii) Give one health problem that has been linked to this natural food additive.

....

c) Substance C is harmful. Draw the hazard symbol you would expect to see on a bottle of substance C.

Q2 The following questions relate to the **periodic table** shown below.

a) Give the symbol for the element in each of the following questions.

i) Identify an element with the same number of outer shell electrons as Se. ....

ii) Which element has the same number of electron shells as Mg? ....

iii) Identify an element that would react vigorously with water to give hydrogen gas. ....

iv) Which element is a green gas that displaces bromine from potassium bromide solution? ....

v) Identify an inert element that is used in electrical discharge tubes. ....

b) Describe how the properties of Group 7 elements change as you go down the group.

....

....

Mixed Questions — C1a Topics 5 & 6

Q3   The equations below represent two different reactions involving **acids**.

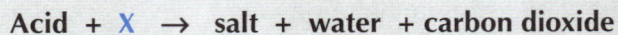

> **Acid + X → salt + water + carbon dioxide**
>
> **Acid + Y → salt + water**

a)   Which substance, X or Y: **i)** is a metal oxide? .... **ii)** is a metal carbonate? ....

b)   Both reactions give out heat. What name is given to this type of reaction? Circle your answer.

exothermic   endothermic

Q4   Look at the different types of **reaction** listed, and decide which type each statement refers to.

thermal decomposition   hydration   dehydration   precipitation

a)   Used to prepare an insoluble salt from two soluble salts. ....

b)   Always endothermic. ....

c)   Always has water as a product. ....

d)   Always has water as a reactant. ....

Q5   **Transition metals**, found in the centre of the periodic table, are typical metals.

a)   Give three properties of copper that make it suitable for use in electrical wiring.

....

b)   **Iron** is extracted from its ore by heating it with carbon monoxide. **Aluminium** is extracted from its ore using electrolysis. **Gold** is usually found by itself in nature.

Put these metals in order of reactivity, beginning with the least reactive.

....

Q6   Jamal is investigating an unknown **metal carbonate**.

a)   When he puts the sample in a Bunsen flame a brick-red colour is seen. Which metal is present?

....

b)   Complete the word equation for the reaction that occurs when a metal carbonate is heated.

metal carbonate → metal .... + ...

c)   Explain how Jamal would collect and test for the gas produced.

....

....

Useful Products from Air and Salt

Q1 Air is a **mixture** of several gases and water vapour.

a) Label the sections of the pie chart with the following gases found in air.

nitrogen   argon   oxygen

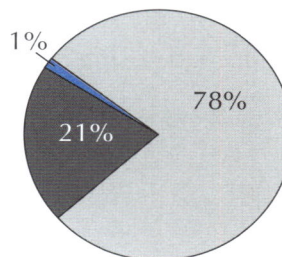

b) What method can be used to separate nitrogen and oxygen in the air?

....

1%
78%
21%

Q2 Complete the passage below by choosing the correct words from each pair.

The boiling point of **nitrogen** / **oxygen** is –196 °C and the boiling point of **nitrogen** / **oxygen** is –187 °C. The gases can be separated by cooling air until it **liquefies** / **solidifies**, then gradually warming it up. When the temperature of the air reaches –196 °C, the **nitrogen** / **oxygen** boils off, but the **nitrogen** / **oxygen** remains liquid — so the gases are separated.

Q3 Oxygen and nitrogen are both used in **industry**. Match them up with their uses.

welding

for making other chemicals

as a rocket fuel

to make ammonia

oxygen

nitrogen

for cooling

hospital use

providing an unreactive atmosphere

crude oil drilling

Q4 Salt, **sodium chloride**, has many uses.

a) Describe how salt is obtained on a large scale in hot countries.

....

b) Where did the layers of underground rock salt in Britain come from?

....

c) i) What is rock salt largely a mixture of? ....

   ii) Suggest one use of rock salt. ....

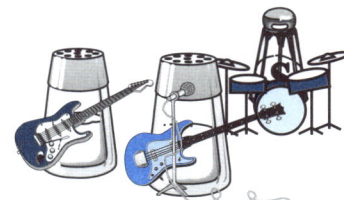

Useful Products from Air and Salt

Q5   The **hydrogen** produced by the electrolysis of **sodium chloride solution** is used in many different ways.

a)   What is made using hydrogen in the Haber process? ....

b)   In what ways is hydrogen used in the metal-working industry?

....

Q6   'Harry's Salt Water Products' is a company that **electrolyses salt water** and sells the products for use in various **industries**. Harry keeps a record of the different amounts sold to the different industries, as shown in the pie chart.

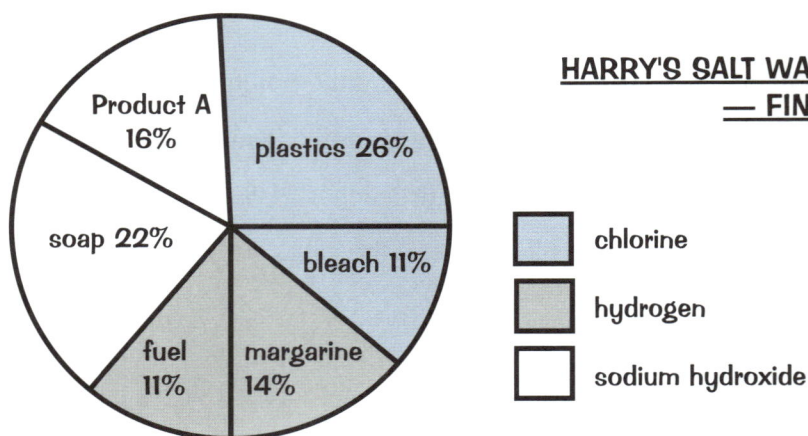

HARRY'S SALT WATER PRODUCTS LTD.
— FINAL USES

Product A 16%
plastics 26%
soap 22%
bleach 11%
fuel 11%
margarine 14%

☐ chlorine
☐ hydrogen
☐ sodium hydroxide

a)   Which industry uses Harry's products the most? Circle the correct answer.

plastics   bleach   margarine   fuel   soap

b)   Which brine product did Harry sell the most of? Circle the correct answer.

chlorine   hydrogen   sodium hydroxide

c)   Product A is made using sodium hydroxide. Suggest what A could be.

....

Q7   Complete the sentences below by circling the correct word(s) from each pair.

a)   Sodium can be extracted by the electrolysis of **salt water** / **molten sodium chloride**.

b)   Electrolysis involves passing **an electrical current** / **a gamma ray** through a substance.

c)   Sodium is used to make **detergents** / **ammonia**.

Top Tips: Remember, **electrolysis** simply means **splitting with electricity**. It's not only used to electrolyse salt water but also to separate loads of metals from their ores, e.g. **aluminium**.

Fractional Distillation of Crude Oil

Q1 Circle the correct words to complete these sentences.

a) Crude oil is a **mixture** / **compound** of different molecules.

b) The molecules in crude oil are **hydrocarbons** / **halogens**.

c) Fractional distillation splits crude oil using a **chemical reaction** / **physical process**.

Q2 The diagram shows a **fractionating column** that is used to distil crude oil.

a) What is done to the crude oil before it enters the column?

....

b) Label the diagram to show where the crude oil enters the column.

c) What happens to the temperature of the crude oil as it rises through the column?

....

d) The fractions separated from the crude oil are constantly tapped off at different levels. What physical state are the following fractions in when they leave the fractionating column? Circle your answer.

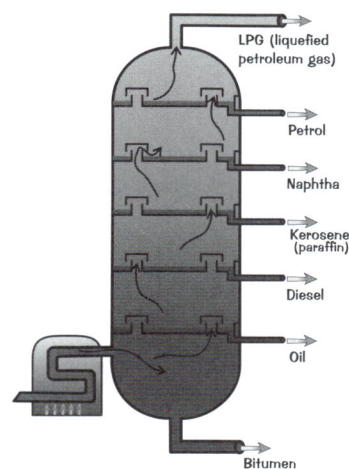

i) Bitumen:

        solid   liquid   gas

ii) Petrol:

        solid   liquid   gas

Q3 Different **fractions** obtained from crude oil have different **uses**.
Match the fractions to their uses. The first one has been done for you.

LPG   starting material in chemical industry

petrol   fuel for non-petrol engines in cars, trucks, trains

naphtha   car fuel

kerosene   road surfacing, roofing asphalt

diesel   bottled gas, pottery and glass-making

oil   jet fuel, paint solvent

bitumen   domestic central heating

phwoar... nice tank, love

Using Hydrocarbons

Q1 **Hydrocarbons** are burnt as fuels.

a) Which two elements are hydrocarbons made up of?

....

b) i) Circle the two products of the complete combustion of a hydrocarbon.

   carbon dioxide   **methane**   **hydrogen**   **water**

ii) What else is released by complete combustion?

....

c) What is needed for a hydrocarbon to burn completely?

....

My favourite few L's

Q2 Natural gas is mostly made up of the hydrocarbon **methane**.

a) Write a word equation for the complete combustion of methane.

....

b) The molecular formula of methane is CH_4.
Complete and **balance** this symbol equation for the complete combustion of methane.

$$CH_4 \ + \ .... \ O_2 \ \rightarrow \ .... \ + \ ....$$

Q3 **Incomplete combustion** can cause problems.

a) Complete this word equation for the incomplete combustion of a hydrocarbon.

hydrocarbon + oxygen → .... + ... + ... + ...

b) Suggest a situation in the home where incomplete combustion might occur.

....

Q4 There are many factors to consider when choosing a **fuel**.

a) Match the following properties of fuels with the type of combustion which increases each property.

Sootiness

Energy value

Toxicity

Complete combustion

Incomplete combustion

b) Name one other property, apart from sootiness, energy value and toxicity,
that should be considered when choosing a fuel.

....

Hydrocarbons and the Environment

Q1 When fossil fuels are burnt they release **carbon dioxide**, **sulphur dioxide** and **nitrogen oxides**. Complete the following sentences by choosing the correct word(s) from each pair.

a) Burning fossil fuels produces mainly **carbon dioxide** / **sulphur dioxide**.

b) The sulphur dioxide comes from **sulphur** / **dioxide** impurities in fossil fuels.

c) The nitrogen oxides are produced by a reaction between nitrogen and oxygen in the **fuel** / **air**, caused by the **heat** / **light** of the burning.

Q2 The gases produced by burning fossil fuels are released into the atmosphere.

a) i) What is produced when sulphur dioxide and nitrogen oxides mix with clouds?

....

ii) What environmental problem does this cause?

....

b) Give the two main **sources** of sulphur dioxide and nitrogen oxides.

....

Q3 Circle the letters next to the sentences below that are **true**.

A Carbon monoxide is produced when hydrocarbons are burnt without enough oxygen.

B Carbon monoxide increases the ability of the blood to carry oxygen around the body.

C Carbon monoxide binds reversibly with haemoglobin.

D Carbon monoxide inhalation can lead to fainting, coma and death.

Q4 **Smog** is a mixture of smoke and fog, and can be deadly.

a) Circle the correct word of each pair in the following sentence:

When **heat** / **sunlight** acts on NO_x / SO_2, photochemical smog is produced.

b) i) Sometimes ground-level ozone is produced. Circle the formula for ozone.

$$O_2 \qquad\qquad O_3 \qquad\qquad O$$

ii) Give one medical problem that ozone can cause. ....

C1b Topic 7 — There's One Earth

The Evolution of the Atmosphere

Q1   Circle the letters next to the sentences below that are **true**.

   A   When the Earth was formed, its surface was molten.

   B   Oxygen eventually began to build up in the Earth's atmosphere,
   mostly due to its release from volcanoes.

   C   When some organisms died and were buried under layers of sediment,
   the carbon they had contained became locked up as fossil fuels.

   D   The development of the ozone layer meant the Earth's temperature became
   suitable for complex organisms to evolve.

Q2   The early atmosphere is thought to have been largely created by the gases released from **volcanoes**.

   a)   Circle the three main gases that the volcanoes released into the atmosphere.

   carbon monoxide   nitrogen   steam   methane   carbon dioxide   oxygen

   b)   Describe how one of these gases changed to form the oceans.

   ....

Q3   The pie charts below show the proportions of different gases in the Earth's
   atmosphere. Pie chart A shows what we think the atmosphere was like
   4500 million years ago. Pie chart B shows the atmosphere as it is **today**.

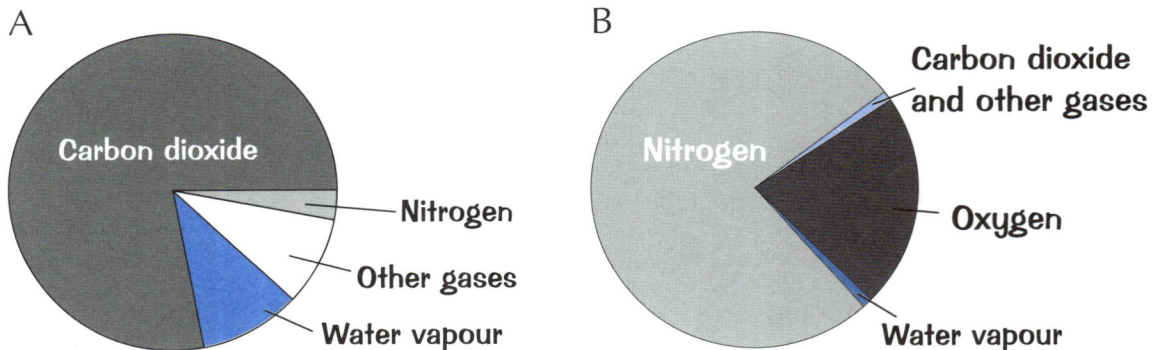

   a)   Describe what has happened to the proportions of the following
   gases in the atmosphere over the last 4500 million years:

   i)   carbon dioxide. ....

   ii)   oxygen. ....

   iii) nitrogen. ....

   b)   What caused the change in carbon dioxide levels?

   ....

   ....

The Evolution of the Atmosphere

Q4   Draw lines to put the statements in the **right order** on the timeline. One has been done for you.

Present

NOT TO SCALE

4600 million years ago

The Earth cools down slightly. A thin crust forms.

The Earth forms. There is lots of volcanic activity.

More complex organisms evolve.

Plant life appears.

Atmosphere is mostly nitrogen and about one-fifth oxygen.

Oxygen builds up due to photosynthesis, and the ozone layer develops.

Q5   The graph shows data on **global temperature** and **concentration of atmospheric CO_2** against time.

a) Mark an X on the temperature line to show when the most recent ice age could have occurred.

An ice age is a time when large areas of the Earth's surface are covered with ice.

b) The Industrial Revolution began around 1850 and people started to burn lots more fossil fuels to provide energy for industry. After 1850, what happens to the:

i) CO_2 line?

....

ii) temperature line?

....

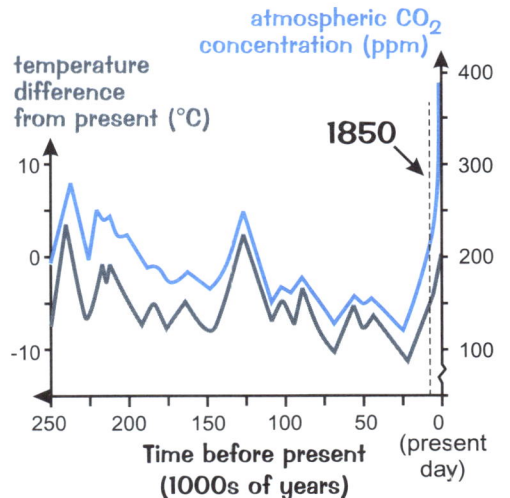

iii) Does this mean that people are definitely causing global warming? Give a reason for your answer.

....

....

Top Tips: So, in its early days the Earth's atmosphere was pretty **different** — loads of CO_2 and not a lot of oxygen. Then good old **plants** came along and sorted everything out ready for the rest of us.

Climate Change

Q1   The idea of **global warming** was first proposed in the 1890s by a Swedish scientist called Arrhenius.

a)   Suggest a reason why it's difficult to be sure that humans are affecting the climate.

....

b)   Circle the correct word(s) from each pair to complete these sentences about global warming:

i)   Most scientists now agree that the world's temperature is **rising** / **falling**.

ii)   The use of **fossil** / **nuclear** fuels is thought to be linked to this change in global temperature.

iii)   When these fuels are burnt they give off **ozone** / **carbon dioxide**, which is a **greenhouse** / **radioactive** gas.

Q2   The diagram shows **radiation** from the Sun entering the Earth's **atmosphere**.

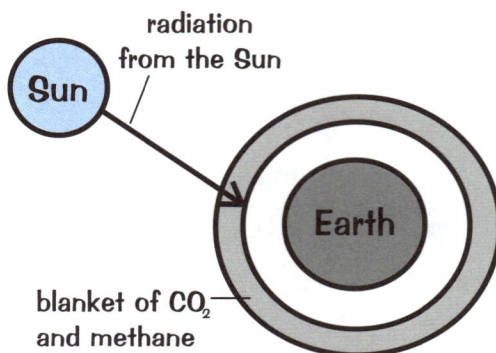

a)   Complete the diagram by showing the path of the radiation after it enters the atmosphere.

b)   What would happen to the radiation from the Sun if the CO_2 and methane weren't there?

....

....

c)   Explain how 'too much' CO_2 and methane in the atmosphere is thought to contribute to global warming.

....

Q3   Carbon dioxide and methane in the atmosphere help to regulate the Earth's temperature.

a)   Circle the statement below that best explains how CO_2 and methane help to regulate the Earth's temperature.

A They absorb heat from the Sun.   **B They keep the polar ice caps from melting.**

C They absorb heat from the Earth.   **D They counteract acid rain.**

b)   What would happen to the temperature of the Earth at night if there was no CO_2 or methane in the Earth's atmosphere?

....

Climate Change

Q4 Many of our everyday actions cause **carbon dioxide** to be released into the atmosphere.

a) Circle the actions that **reduce** the amount of carbon dioxide released.

Flying to a holiday destination abroad rather than taking the train to the seaside.

Walking or taking the bus to school instead of being driven.

Leaving the light on when you leave the room instead of switching it off.

Leaving the TV on standby all night rather than switching it off.

b) Explain how buying food that has been grown abroad and flown to this country, instead of buying local produce, affects how much CO_2 is produced.

....

....

Q5 Scientists try to **predict** what the Earth's **temperature** will be in the future using computer models. Tick the boxes to show whether the following statements are **true** or **false**.

	True	False
a) Computer modelling uses data collected from thousands of monitoring stations all over the world.	☐	☐
b) Computers models use millions of calculations to improve the data entered into them.	☐	☐
c) Computer models are based on assumptions, so their predictions may not always be true.	☐	☐
d) Small errors in early calculations will disappear as the predictions go further and further forward in time.	☐	☐

Q6 The **Kyoto Protocol** is an agreement made by over 160 countries to reduce CO_2, methane and other greenhouse gas emissions by 5% by the year **2012**.

a) Describe one way that countries could reduce the amount of **fossil fuels** they burn.

....

b) Scientists have used computer models to predict that if the Kyoto Protocol is upheld the effect of global warming between 1990 and 2050 will be reduced by 0.2 °C.
Give a reason why this prediction may not be accurate.

....

....

Recycling

Q1 Choose the correct word(s) from each pair to complete the definition of **sustainable development**.

Sustainable development meets the **needs** / **wants** of today's population without

aiding / **harming** the ability of future generations to meet **their own** / **our** needs.

Q2 Tick the correct boxes to show whether the following statements are **true** or **false**.

		True	False
a)	Recycling could help to prevent further increases in greenhouse gas levels.	☐	☐
b)	It is important to recycle metal because there is a finite amount available.	☐	☐
c)	Recycling costs nothing and has huge benefits for the environment.	☐	☐

Q3 Give three advantages of **recycling** materials such as **metals**, **paper** and **glass**.

1. ....

2. ....

3. ....

Q4 Below is some information about **aluminium**, a widely used metal today.

- **Bauxite (aluminium ore) gives 1 kg of aluminium for every 4 kg of bauxite mined.**
- **Bauxite mines are often located in rainforests.**
- **Extracting aluminium from bauxite requires huge quantities of electricity.**
- **An aluminium can weighs about 20 g.**

a) i) On average, each Australian used about 150 aluminium cans in 2002.
How many kilograms of aluminium were present in the cans each person used?

....

ii) If none of the cans were made from recycled aluminium, how much bauxite would have been mined to supply each Australian with aluminium cans in 2002?

....

iii) The population of Australia in 2002 was approximately 20 million. How many tonnes of bauxite were needed to supply all of Australia with non-recycled aluminium cans in 2002?

240 tonnes   **2400 tonnes**   **24 000 tonnes**   **240 000 tonnes**

Don't forget,
1 tonne = 1000 kg.

b) Outline an environmental consequence of:

i) Mining the bauxite. ....

ii) Extracting the aluminium. ....

iii) Not recycling the cans. ....

Sustainable Development

Q1   **Hydrogen** is often talked about as the 'fuel of the future'.

a)   What is the only product produced when hydrogen is burnt? ....

b)   Why is it better for the environment if hydrogen rather than petrol is burnt?

....

....

c)   Explain the problems that will have to be overcome before the public will be able to use hydrogen-powered vehicles on a large scale.

....

....

....

Think about storage of hydrogen and the costs involved.

Q2   **Biogas** is an alternative to natural gas, a fossil fuel. Tick the boxes to show whether the following statements are **true** or **false**.

		True	False
a)	Biogas is mostly a mixture of methane and carbon dioxide.	☐	☐
b)	Microorganisms are used to decompose animal waste and dead plants to create products such as biogas.	☐	☐
c)	Burning biogas produces lots of particulates and releases large amounts of sulphur dioxide and nitrogen oxides.	☐	☐
d)	Biogas can be used to power a turbine and generate electricity.	☐	☐

Q3   The diagram shows the production and use of one type of **biogas**.

a)   Label the diagram by writing the correct letter next to each arrow:

   A CO_2 released into atmosphere

   B biogas generator

   C animal waste

   D CO_2 absorbed by grass during photosynthesis

   E methane $\rightarrow CO_2$

b)   Explain why biogas is a renewable fuel.

....

....

....

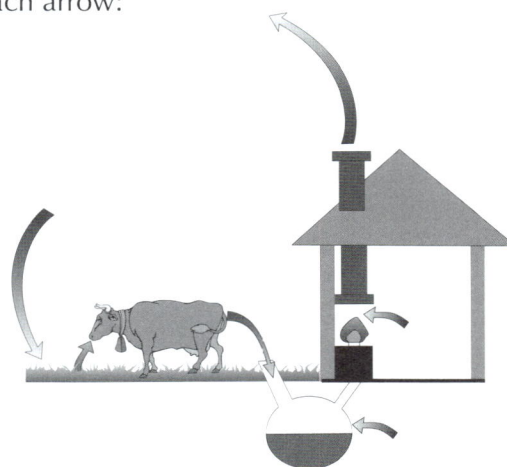

Sustainable Development

Q4   In Brazil, **ethanol** produced by **fermenting sugar cane** is a popular fuel for vehicles. Choose the correct words from each pair to complete the following sentences.

a)   Ethanol is a hydrocarbon so produces **carbon dioxide and water** / **carbon monoxide and sulphuric acid** when it's burnt with plenty of oxygen.

b)   Gasohol is a mixture of ethanol and petrol — using gasohol instead of pure petrol means that **more** / **less** crude oil is needed.

c)   While the sugar cane used to make ethanol is growing, it absorbs **carbon dioxide** / **oxygen** from the air during photosynthesis.

d)   Using gasohol increases the amount of carbon dioxide in the atmosphere **less** / **more** than using pure petrol.

Q5   **Alternative fuels** have advantages and disadvantages compared with traditional fossil fuels.

a)   Match each of the fuels below with an advantage and a disadvantage of using it.

The raw materials used to make this fuel are cheap and readily available.

Biogas

This fuel is expensive and difficult to store.

The raw materials used to make part of this fuel absorb carbon dioxide as they grow.

Hydrogen fuel

Large areas of fertile land are used to produce the raw materials needed to make this fuel.

The only waste product released when this fuel is burnt is water.

Gasohol

A lot of energy is required to distil the ethanol in this fuel.

b)   Imagine you are writing a leaflet promoting the use of alternative fuels as a way of achieving sustainable development.

i)   Give one advantage **not** mentioned in part a) that you could use in your argument.

....

ii)   Suggest a point **not** mentioned in part a) that someone who disagrees with you might give.

....

Top Tips: **Sustainable development** isn't all about loving trees and hugging bunnies, but about being sensible now so that our descendants don't have to live on raw rat meat and live underground to hide from all the **pollution** we've left behind. So think about them when you leave your TV on standby.

Novel Properties

Q1   **KEVLAR**® is an extremely useful material which is used for many **different purposes**.

Match the uses of KEVLAR® given below to the **properties** that make it suitable for each use.

Bulletproof vests

Glass-workers' gloves

Firefighters' helmets

Canoes

Light / strong

Heat-resistant / strong / light

Cut-resistant (strong) / light / flexible

Soft / flexible / light / strong

Q2   The glue used on **Post-it**® **Notes** was invented by accident when scientists were trying to create a new glue to use on sticky tape.

a)   What property of the new glue made it unsuitable for sticky tape?

....

b)   Why is this property of the glue ideal for its eventual use on Post-it® Notes?

....

Q3   **Thinsulate**™ is a new smart material.

a)   Complete the following sentence describing how Thinsulate™ works.

Thinsulate™ is an excellent **thermal** / **electrical** insulator because

it contains very **thin** / **thick** fibres that trap a lot of **water** / **air**.

b)   Give one practical use of Thinsulate™. ....

Q4   GORE-TEX® is a brand of fabric. The pores in the **PTFE membrane** in **GORE-TEX**® are much larger than **water molecules**, but much smaller than **water droplets**.

a)   Explain the importance of this pore size in the function of clothing made from GORE-TEX®.

....

....

b)   As well as the PTFE membrane, GORE-TEX® includes a layer of another fabric, such as nylon. Explain why this is necessary.

....

Smart Materials

Q1 **Nitinol** is a shape memory alloy which has some unusual properties.

a) Circle the correct words to complete the following paragraph about nitinol.

Nitinol is a **metal** / **plastic** that can be bent and twisted like rubber. If it is bent too far, nitinol will **stay bent** / **crack**. However, if it's **heated** / **cooled** beyond a certain temperature, it goes back to a **remembered** / **new** shape.

b) Suggest a use for nitinol.

....

Q2 The packaging around some **fresh sausages** has a coloured dot on it that gradually gets **darker**. The **speed** at which this happens depends on the **temperature**, as shown in the graph below.

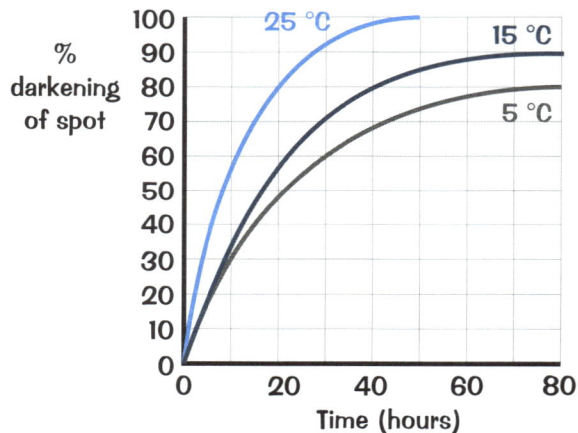

a) What is this sort of packaging called? ....

b) When the dot is more than **80% dark**, the food is no longer safe to eat. The graph shows that the food is safe to eat for up to **80 hours** when kept at **5 °C**. For how long is it safe to eat when kept:

i) at 15 °C? ....

ii) at 25 °C? ....

c) Complete the sentences below to explain how the packaging works.

i) The coloured dot contains **dye** / **silica** which changes colour **faster** / **more slowly** as it gets warmer.

ii) The dot shows whether the food has been warm for long enough for **microbes** / **antibodies** to grow.

C1b Topic 8 — Designer Products

Smart Materials

Q3   Julia is investigating how the **amount of water** affects the amount of **mould** that grows on bread.

She takes three slices of **bread** and seals them in airtight jars. One jar contains just the bread, one also contains some silica gel and the third contains some fresh orange peel. After a week she estimates the amount of **mould** on each of the slices of bread. The results are shown below.

Contents of jar	% Surface of bread with mould
Bread and silica gel	5
Bread only	25
Bread and orange peel	65

Silica gel is a chemical that absorbs water. Fresh orange peel is known to gradually release water.

a)   Name one variable she should control in this experiment.

....

b)   Why do the jars have to be sealed?

....

c)   What can Julia conclude?

....

Q4   **Smart materials** can change their properties depending on the external conditions. Match each of the smart materials below with a product they would be suitable for.

A dye that changes from red to green when it is cooled below a certain temperature.

sunglasses

A dye that becomes more transparent as the light intensity decreases.

drinks cans and bottles to show when they're cold enough to drink

Q5   Tick the boxes to show whether the following statements about **oxygen scavengers** are true or false.

	True	False
a) Oxygen scavengers are chemicals that react with oxygen.	☐	☐
b) Oxygen scavengers add oxygen to the inside of packaging.	☐	☐
c) Oxygen scavengers make it harder for microbes to grow inside packaging.	☐	☐
d) Food packaged with oxygen scavengers needs more preservatives.	☐	☐

Nanotechnology

Q1 Tick the boxes to show whether the following statements about **nanoparticles** are true or false.

		True	False
a)	Nanoparticles are made out of the smart material nano.	☐	☐
b)	Nanoparticles are really tiny particles, 1-100 nm across.	☐	☐
c)	Nanoparticles have the same properties as the bulk chemicals they're made from.	☐	☐

Q2 Use the entries provided to complete the table below to show how **nanoparticles** can have different **properties** to the bulk chemical they're made from.

Prevents viruses getting into cells   Doesn't reflect visible light   Gold-coloured

CHEMICAL	NANOPARTICLE PROPERTY	BULK' CHEMICAL PROPERTY
Zinc oxide		Reflects visible light
Silver		Doesn't affect microbes
Gold	Red or purple-coloured	

Q3 **Nanoparticles** have the potential to be extremely **useful** materials.

a) Match the following nanoparticles with their uses:

gold nanoparticles   sunscreen

zinc oxide nanoparticles   medicine

silver nanoparticles   nanowires

b) **i)** What is the difference between nanowires and ordinary wires?

....

ii) What does this mean for computer chips?

....

Nanotechnology

Q4 Particles of **titanium dioxide** are used as a pigment in white paint because they reflect visible light very strongly.

Nanoparticles of titanium dioxide <u>don't reflect</u> visible light.

a) **i)** Write the letters A-C below to order the following particle sizes from smallest to largest:

A 0.1-5 μm   **B** 1-100 nm   **C** 1-10 cm

...................' ....' ....

ii) Which of these sizes would you expect the titanium dioxide particles in white paint to be? ....

b) **Nanoparticles** of titanium dioxide are used in sunscreens. Match the properties of titanium dioxide nanoparticles to their benefit in sunscreen.

don't reflect visible light

leaves no marks on the skin

reflect UV light

not dissolved by sweat

insoluble in water

prevents harmful rays reaching the skin

stable under UV light

properties not changed by sunlight

Q5 Nanocomposites are materials that combine nanomaterials with other substances.

a) What can adding a nanomaterial do to the properties of a substance?

....

b) A concrete nanocomposite has been developed for use in building.

i) Which nanomaterial does this nanocomposite contain?

....

A nanocampsite

ii) What benefits are there in using the nanocomposite?

....

Top Tips: The discovery of all these bizarre properties of nanoparticles opened up huge new areas to investigate. Putting familiar materials to novel uses means technology that was once science-fiction is now a real possibility — all thanks to a bunch of tiny little particles. Hooray for nanoparticles.

Beer and Wine

Q1   Circle the correct word from each pair to complete the sentences.

a)   Fermentation is used to turn sugars / yeast into ethanol.

b)   The fermentation reaction happens due to bacteria / enzymes found in yeast.

c)   The temperature needs to be carefully controlled during the reaction:

i)   if it is too cold / hot the reaction is very slow.

ii)   if it is too cold / hot the enzymes are destroyed.

Q2   Mark met his friend John as he was leaving the pub. John had been **drinking** for several hours, and Mark noticed that he was **swaying** and that he **stumbled** several times as he walked away.

a)   Match each man to the characteristics he is more likely to display.

responsible sexual behaviour

lack of inhibition   impaired judgement

aggression

self-control   problems with balance and coordination

Mark   **John**

b)   Use one or more of the characteristics from part a) to explain who should **drive** the friends home.

....

....

Q3   Answer the following questions about **fermentation** by circling A, B or C for each part.

a)   Which of the following is the correct equation for the production of ethanol?

A   glucose → ethanol + oxygen

B   glucose → ethanol + carbon dioxide

C   fructose → ethanol + carbon dioxide

b)   What is the name of the enzyme in yeast? Circle the correct letter.

A Ethanoate   B Fermentase   C Zymase

c)   The fermentation reaction stops when the concentration of ethanol reaches about 10-20%. How is the concentration of ethanol increased to make drinks such as whisky or vodka?

A Distillation   B Foundationalisation   C Fermentallation

Beer and Wine

Q4 Tick the boxes to show whether the following statements about **fermentation** are true or false.

	True	False
a) It is important to allow oxygen to enter the fermentation process.	☐	☐
b) Oxygen converts ethanol to ethanoic acid.	☐	☐
c) Different types of alcoholic drinks are made using sugars from different sources.	☐	☐
d) Fermentation stops when all the enzymes in the yeast are used up.	☐	☐

Q5 Excessive **alcohol** intake can have **damaging effects** on the human body.

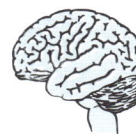

a) What effect does alcohol have on the nervous system?

....

b) Which organ is often damaged by excessive alcohol intake?

....

c) Which of these are economic costs to society of excessive drinking? Circle the correct answer(s).

lost working days

treatment of drinking-related accidents and illness on the NHS

police time wasted dealing with drunks

Q6 Alcohol can be **addictive**, and an addiction to alcohol is known as **alcoholism**. Explain how alcoholism can cause the following effects:

a) Damage to a person's health.

....

b) Family breakdown.

....

c) Unemployment.

....

Top Tips: There's some evidence that a glass of red wine with your dinner may be good for you. In the newspaper headlines, that might appear as "Drinking's good for you", but never forget — drinking to excess can be a **disaster** — for your health, your family, your career, the world...

Emulsifiers and Properties

Q1   Match up the following **products** with a **material** they could be made out of, and the **properties** of the material that makes it suitable for making each product.

Electrical wire		Wool		Flexible, good conductor of electricity
Scarf		Copper		Rigid, poor conductor of electricity
Light switch		Plastic		Flexible, soft, poor conductor of heat

Q2   Jeremy is making some **mayonnaise** by mixing together some oil and lemon juice in a jar. After five minutes he notices the mixture has separated into two layers.

a)   Explain why the mixture has separated into layers.

....

....

b)   What sort of substance could Jeremy add to the jar to make the mayonnaise usable?

....

Q3   The diagram shows an **emulsifier** in action.

a)   Complete the diagram by labelling the following:

hydrophobic part   oil

emulsifier

hydrophilic part   water

b)   Emulsifiers are molecules with one part that's attracted to water and one bit that's attracted to oil. Circle the correct word to complete each sentence.

   i)   The bit that's attracted to water is called **hydrophilic** / **hydrophobic**.

   ii)   The bit that's attracted to oil is called **hydrophilic** / **hydrophobic**.

c)   Describe what happens when oil and water are shaken together with an emulsifier.

....

....

Q4   Indicate whether the following statements are **true** or **false**.

		True	False
a)	Emulsifiers help to make oil and water separate out.	☐	☐
b)	An emulsion is made up of droplets of solid suspended in a liquid.	☐	☐
c)	The 'tail' of a molecule of emulsifier is the hydrophobic part.	☐	☐

Mixed Questions — C1b Topics 7 & 8

Q1 Complete the table below by entering one **use** of each material, and the **property** of the material that makes it suitable for that use.

sunscreen   sportswear   bike frames   *very strong and light*   *reflect UV light*   *very stretchy and light*

Material	Use	Property
Carbon fibre		
LYCRA®		
Zinc oxide nanoparticles		

Q2 One problem with fossil fuels like petrol is that they will run out one day. However other more sustainable fuels, such as **gasohol** — a mix of petrol and ethanol, are available.

a) The **ethanol** in gasohol is often produced by the fermentation of **sugar cane**, which is grown on large plantations. Give one advantage and one disadvantage of growing the raw materials for a fuel.

i) advantage: ....

ii) disadvantage: ....

b) Give the word equation for the fermentation of **glucose** in sugar into **ethanol**.

....

Q3 The Earth's **atmosphere** has evolved over **millions of years**.

a) Give two differences between the early atmosphere, before green plants evolved, and today's atmosphere.

1. ....

2. ....

b) Choose the correct word(s) from each pair to complete the following sentences.

Greenhouse / **Noble** gases in the Earth's atmosphere form **a conducting** / **an insulating** layer

that reduces the amount of heat from the Sun that is radiated back **into space** / **to Earth**.

The amount of carbon dioxide and methane in the atmosphere is **rising** / **falling** rapidly.

The **density** / **temperature** of the atmosphere is also **rising** / **falling**, causing concern.

c) Earth's oceans were formed as water vapour in the atmosphere cooled and condensed. Seawater can be 'split' into useful substances, e.g. hydrogen, by electrolysis. Outline how electrolysis works.

....

d) Fuel cells use hydrogen to make electricity, and can be used to power vehicles. Give one benefit of using hydrogen fuel cells instead of petrol.

....

Mixed Questions — C1b Topics 7 & 8

Q4   Glyn is making a salad for his dinner. However, the **packaging** of his salad dressing shows that the dressing is no longer safe to eat.

a)   The intelligent packaging contains a spot of dye that changes colour faster the warmer it gets. Explain how this is useful.

....

....

b)   Glyn decides to make his own dressing. He mixes some olive oil and vinegar in a bowl.

i)   What will happen if the oil and vinegar are left for a few minutes?

....

ii)   Glyn stirs some mustard powder into the bowl. The oil forms small droplets and mixes with the vinegar. What sort of substance is the mustard powder?

....

c)   Glyn usually has a few glasses of wine with his dinner, but his doctor has recommended he should cut down on alcoholic drinks. Suggest a harmful effect of drinking to excess.

....

Q5   Describe two benefits of recycling.

1. ....

2. ....

Q6   **Crude oil** can be separated in the laboratory using small-scale **fractional distillation**, giving the fractions shown in the table.

fraction	flammability
petrol	very flammable, clean yellow flame
naphtha	quite flammable, some smoke
kerosene	harder to light, quite smoky flame

a)   i)   Which of the fractions in the table would make the most useful fuel? Give a reason for your answer.

....

ii)   Give a common use of one of the fractions in the table.

....

b)   i)   Propane is a hydrocarbon with the molecular formula C_3H_8.
Write a balanced symbol equation for the **complete combustion** of propane.

....

ii)   What two additional products would you expect from **incomplete** combustion?

....

c)   Outline two environmental problems that are caused by burning hydrocarbons.

....

Electric Current

Q1   Use the words in the box to fill in the gaps. Use each word once only.

> more   voltage   resistance   less   current   force

a)   The flow of electrons round a circuit is called the ....

b)   .... is the .... that pushes the current round the circuit.

c)   If you increase the voltage, ... current will flow.

d)   If you increase the ...., ... current will flow.

Q2   Here are three different circuits, **A – C**. All the **cells** and **resistors** are **identical**.

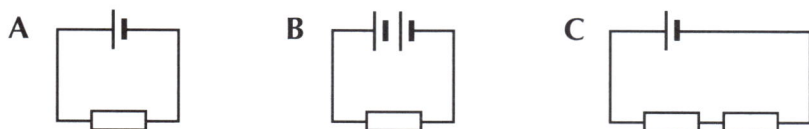

Write down the letters representing the circuits in order of **increasing current**. ..../ ..../ ....

Q3   The diagram shows three traces on the same **CRO**. The settings are the **same** in each case.

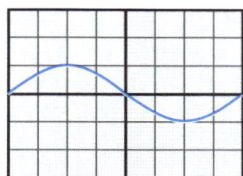  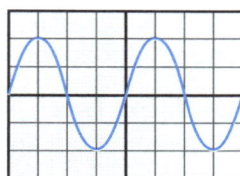 

A	B	C

Write down the letter of the trace that shows:

a)   the highest AC frequency ..../   b)   direct current ..../

c)   the lowest AC voltage ..../   d)   the current from a battery ....

Q4   Scientists **decided** the convention for which way current flows around an electrical circuit before electrons were discovered.

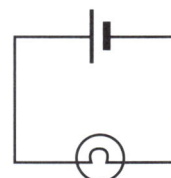

a)   Draw arrows on the diagram on the right to show the direction of **conventional current**.

b)   **Which way** would the **electrons** be moving? Circle the correct answer.

   clockwise   anticlockwise

Generating Electricity

Q1 Select the correct word from each pair to complete these sentences.

> You can create a voltage in a coil of wire by **holding** / **rotating** a magnet near the wire. This is called **electromagnetic** / **superconductive** induction. The coil of wire must be part of a **complete** / **incomplete** circuit for current to flow. **A direct** / **An alternating** current is generated.

Q2 The diagrams below show the CRO traces produced when a **coil of wire** is **rotated** around a **magnet**.

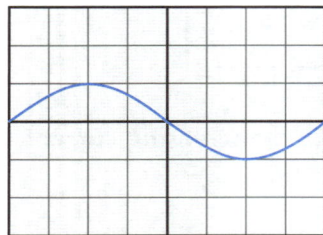

A

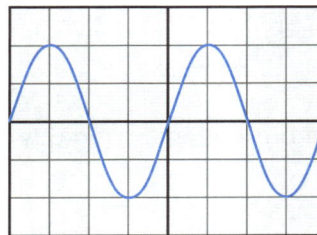

B

a) Which trace (A or B) shows the coil of wire being turned more quickly? ....

b) What sort of current is being produced in both traces? ....

c) Apart from rotating the coil of wire faster, give three other things you could do to make the maximum voltage **larger**.

1. ....

2. ....

3. ....

Q3 The lights on Sebastian's bicycle are powered by a **dynamo**. Tick the boxes to show whether each statement is **true** or **false**.

	True	False
a) As the wheels of Sebastian's bike turn, they rotate a magnet inside the dynamo.	☐	☐
b) When Sebastian cycles faster the lights will dim.	☐	☐
c) The dynamo needs a battery to produce electricity.	☐	☐
d) When Sebastian stops at traffic lights, his bicycle lights will go out.	☐	☐

Generating Electricity

Q4 Decide whether the following AC generators would produce a **higher**, a **lower** or **the same** voltage as the generator in the box. Circle the correct answer in each case.

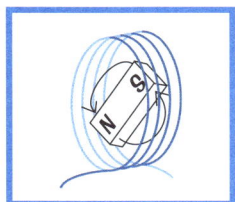

a) More coils   higher / lower / the same

b) Stronger magnet   higher / lower / the same

c) Slower rotation   higher / lower / the same

Q5 Moving a **magnet** inside a **coil of wire** produces a trace on a cathode ray oscilloscope.

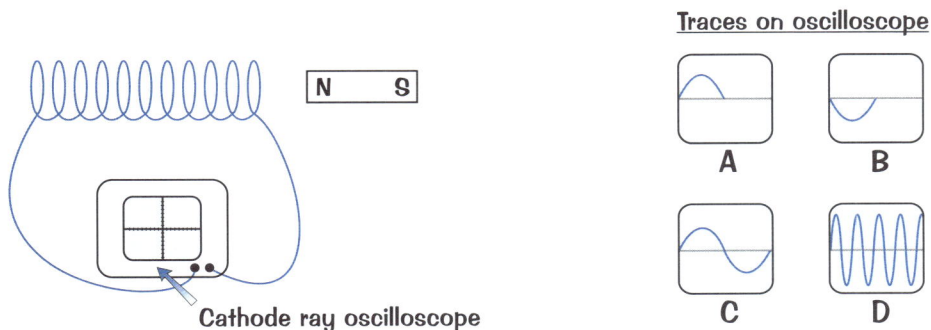

N   S

Cathode ray oscilloscope

Traces on oscilloscope

A   B

C   D

a) When the magnet was pushed inside the coil from the right hand end, trace A was produced on the screen. Write the letter of the trace that each of the following actions would produce:

i) **The magnet is pushed into the coil from the left-hand end.**

ii) **The magnet is pushed into the coil from the right-hand end then pulled out again.**

b) Describe how trace D could be produced.

....

....

Top Tips: You can tell why people thought electricity was magic in the olden days — wave a magnet near some wire and hey presto... you get some electricity. Make sure you know what four factors can make the voltage generated change — and you'll generate lots of marks.

Current, Voltage and Resistance

Q1   Match up these items from a standard test circuit with the **correct description** and **symbol**.

ITEM	DESCRIPTION	SYMBOL
Cell	The item you're testing.	
Variable Resistor	Provides the voltage.	
Component	Used to alter the current.	
Voltmeter	Measures the current.	
Ammeter	Measures the voltage.	

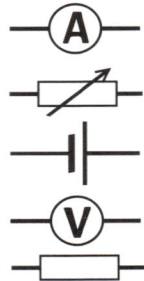

Q2   Indicate whether these statements are **true** or **false**.

                                                                 True   False

a)   An ammeter should always be connected in parallel with a component.   ☐ ☐

b)   A voltmeter should always be connected in series with a component.   ☐ ☐

c)   The resistance of a filament lamp changes as it gets hot.   ☐ ☐

d)   For most of a cell's 'life', it supplies a constant voltage.   ☐ ☐

Q3   Match the correct label to each of the **V-I graphs** below.

a)
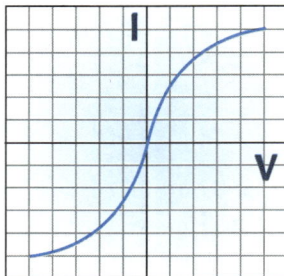

RESISTOR

FILAMENT LAMP

b)
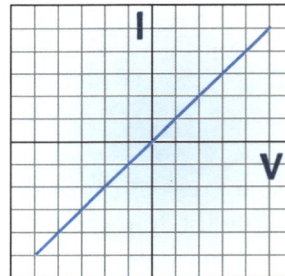

Q4   Complete these sentences by circling the correct word from each pair.

a)   When the voltage applied to a component is increased,
the **current** / **resistance** passing through it increases too.

b)   The current is proportional to the **voltage** / **resistance**
so long as the **temperature** / **pressure** stays the same.

c)   The resistance of a filament lamp varies because its **temperature** / **mass**
varies with the current flowing through it.

Current, Voltage and Resistance

Q5   The **formula** relating resistance, voltage and current is shown below.

$$V = I \times R$$

a)   Calculate the voltage across a 3 Ω resistor if a current of 2 A is flowing through it.

....

b) **i)**   Rearrange the formula to make current, I, the subject.

....

The subject of the formula at the moment is voltage, V.

ii)   Calculate the current through a 2 Ω resistor when the voltage across it is 4 V.

....

c)   Calculate the resistance of resistor R in the circuit shown.

....

3 A

R

6 V

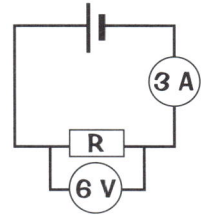

Q6   The graph below shows V-I curves for **four resistors**.

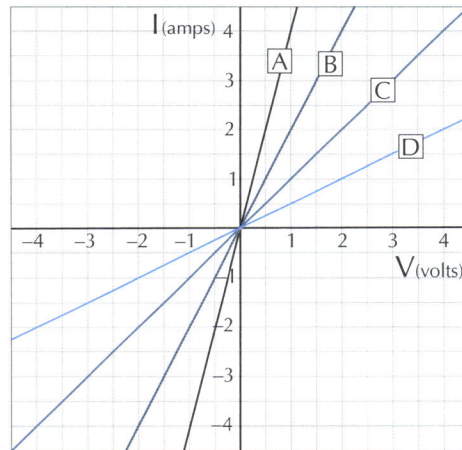

The steeper the graph, the lower the resistance.

a)   Which resistor has the highest resistance? ....

b)   What is the current through **resistor A** when the voltage across it is 0.5 volts?

....

c)   What is the voltage across **resistor B** when the current through it is 3 amps?

....

d)   Find the resistance of **resistor C**.

....

Varying Resistance and Sensors

Q1 Tick the boxes to show whether the following statements are **true** or **false**.

		True	False
a)	LDRs and thermistors are types of variable resistor.	☐	☐
b)	An LDR has a high resistance in very bright light.	☐	☐
c)	The resistance of a thermistor increases as the temperature decreases.	☐	☐
d)	An LDR could be part of a useful thermostat.	☐	☐

Q2 After each of the following sentences, write **LDR** if it's about an LDR, **thermistor** if it's about a thermistor, or **both** if it applies to both.

a) Could be used as part of a thermostat. ....

b) Could be used as a light sensor. ....

c) Changes its resistance in response to conditions around it. ....

d) Would have a lower resistance in a warmer room. ....

e) Would have a high resistance in a dark room. ....

CENSORED

Q3 Sarah monitored the temperature inside her fridge over 6 hours using a thermistor and a data-logging system. A graph of her results is shown below.

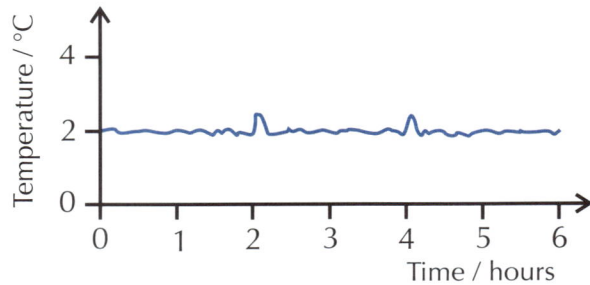

a) i) What happened to the temperature just after **2 hours** and **4 hours**?

....

ii) What might have caused this?

....

b) The data-logging system recorded the temperature inside the fridge at 1 minute intervals for 6 hours. Give a reason why you **couldn't** carry out this experiment using a normal hand-held thermometer.

....

....

Varying Resistance and Sensors

Q4   A camera's **shutter** controls how much light enters the lens. Many modern cameras automatically adjust how long the shutter stays open, so that the right amount of light reaches the lens.

a)   What type of variable resistor is used in camera shutter circuits?

....

b)   Complete the following sentences to explain how the camera shutter works:

i)   In low light, the resistance of the LDR is **high / low**, so the shutter stays open for a long time.

ii)   In bright light, the resistance of the LDR is **high / low**, so the shutter stays open for a short time.

Q5   Helen set up an experiment to see how the **resistance** of an **LDR** varies with **light intensity**. Here are her results:

Light intensity / W/m²	5	10	20	30	40	50
Resistance / Ω	6000	3500	2000	1500	1200	1000

a)   Use Helen's results in the table above to complete the graph below.

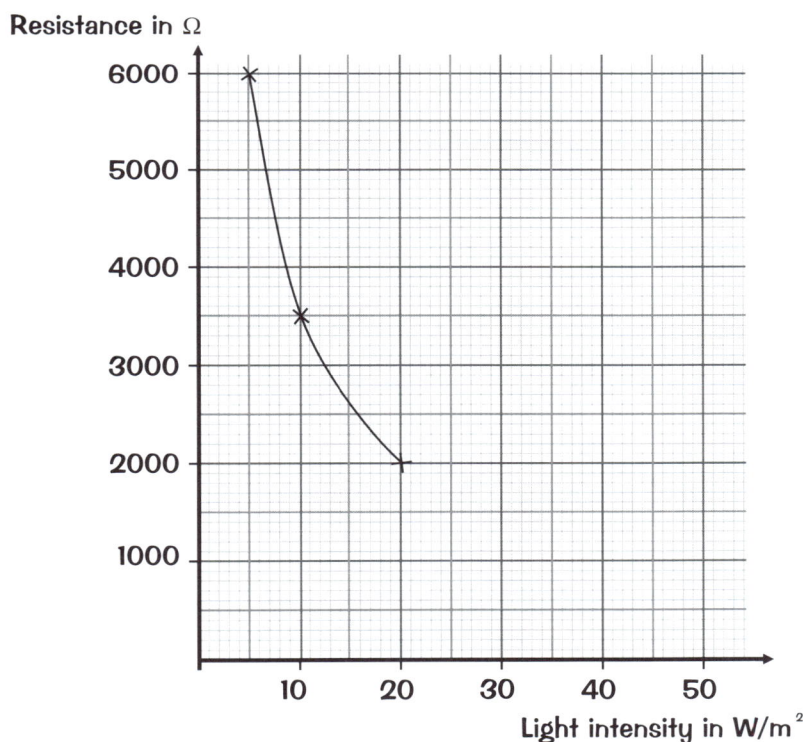

b)   i)   Use the graph to find the resistance when the light intensity is 15 W/m².

....

ii)   Use the graph to find the light intensity when the resistance is 1700 Ω.

....

Batteries and Their Uses

Q1   Complete the following passage by choosing the correct word(s) from each pair.

> Dry-cell batteries are **cheaper** / **more expensive** and last longer than a single charge of a rechargeable battery, but once they have gone flat they have to be **recharged** / **disposed of**. This can be a waste of resources but there are ways of **recycling** / **reusing** them.

Q2   Many modern devices like mobile phones use **rechargeable** batteries.

  a)   Give **one** advantage of using rechargeable instead of dry-cell batteries.

      ....

  b)   Some rechargeable batteries contain a highly toxic chemical called cadmium.
How must these batteries be disposed of?

      ....

Q3   How long a battery lasts depends on the current it's supplying and its **capacity**.

  a)   Use the words below to fill in the blanks and complete the definition of battery capacity.

         current   **time**   **amp-hours**   **hours**

      Capacity (in ....) = ... (in A) × .... (in ....)

  b)   Match the batteries below with their capacities in amp-hours:

     i)   A car battery that can supply a current of 5 A for 15 hours.

     ii) A calculator battery that can supply a current of 0.05 A for 30 hours.

     iii) The battery in a remote-controlled car that can supply a current of 2 A for 3 hours.

        1.5 A h   **6 A h**   **75 A h**

Q4   The two **batteries** shown have different capacities. Complete the sentences below about them.

  a) **i)** Battery A can supply a current of 3 A for

          .... hours.

     ii) Battery B can supply a current of 2 A for

          .... hours.

         Battery A   **Battery B**
         Capacity: 24 A h   **Capacity: 12 A h**

  b) **i)** Battery A can supply a current of .... A for 4 hours.

     ii) Battery B can supply a current of .... A for 8 hours.

Batteries and Their Uses

Q5   Dura-batt pride themselves on producing long-life batteries. The graph shows the results when their best battery provides a current of **1.5 A** until it goes flat.

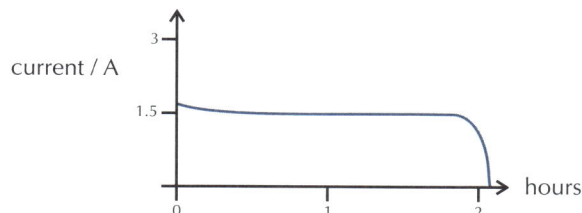

a)   To the nearest hour, for how long was the battery able to supply a current of 1.5 A?

....

b)   Calculate the **capacity** of the battery in amp-hours.

....

c)   For how long would you expect the battery to supply a current of **3 A**?

....

Q6   Simon is a robot geek and is going to compete on 'Robot Legends'. He needs to find out how much it will cost to power his robot, which needs a total battery capacity of **30 A h**.

a)   The robot would need 20 dry-cell batteries with a capacity of 1.5 A h.
One dry-cell battery costs **£1.50**. What would be the total cost of
powering the robot with dry-cell batteries?

....

b)   If Simon uses a rechargeable battery, he will need to recharge it
before each of the 10 rounds.

    i)   The cost of electricity is **10p** for each recharge. How much would it cost for all the recharging?

....

    ii)   The uncharged battery costs **£4.00** to buy.
How much would it cost in total to power the robot using this battery?

....

c)   Because Simon is pretty broke, he wants to power his robot as **cheaply** as possible.
Circle the type of battery he should use.

            dry-cell battery   **rechargeable battery**

Top Tips: As someone once said, rechargeable or dry-cell — that is the question. Anyway, make sure you know the pros and cons of each type, and how to work out battery capacity.

New Technology and the Modern World

Q1   Electricity has transformed many aspects of everyday life. Connect the boxes below to show how.

candle, lantern

washing by hand

coal or wood-burning stove

board games, cards, books

writing letters

salting, pickling, ice-houses

light bulb

electric oven

telephones, mobile phones, e-mails

washing machine

freezer, fridge

TV, stereo, computer games

Q2   Telephones and the internet have completely changed the way people **communicate** over **long distances**.

a)   Give an example of how this has been a change for the better.

....

b)   Give an example of how this change could be damaging.

....

Q3   The **processing power** of computers is changing as technology advances.

a)   Complete the following paragraph by choosing the correct word(s) from each pair.

> The processing power of a computer depends on how many **electric circuits** / **dry-cell batteries** can fit inside it. Modern processor chips are made of **silicon** / **cadmium** with circuits etched on using **nanotools** / **light**. The decreasing size of electrical components means that the processing speed of computers has **increased** / **decreased** in recent years.

b)   Suggest two possible ways that electric circuits may be made in the future, so that even faster, more powerful computers can be created.

1. ....

2. ....

New Technology and the Modern World

Q4 The graph below shows how the number of **transistors** that fit onto a processing chip has changed since 1990.

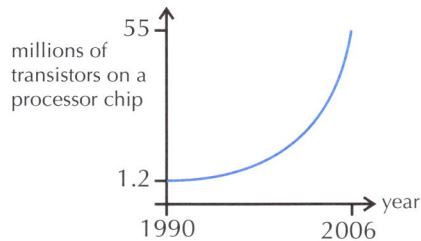

millions of transistors on a processor chip

55

1.2

1990   2006   year

a) Complete the following sentences describing the trend shown on the graph:

The number of transistors that fit on a processing chip has increased / decreased **since 1990. The rate of change has got** faster and faster / slower and slower **over this period.**

b) Why is the size of electrical circuits on processing chips important?

....

....

c) Do you think the number of transistors that can be fitted onto a processing chip will carry on increasing according to the current trend forever? Give a reason for your answer.

....

Q5 The graph below shows how the **processing speed** of computers has increased since 1990.

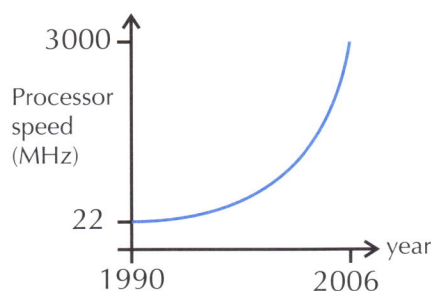

3000

Processor speed (MHz)

22

1990   2006   year

a) Suggest a reason why the processing speed has increased since 1990.

....

b) Describe how the **rate** of increase in processing speed has changed since 1990.

....

c) Suggest a use of computers that has benefited from the increased processing speed.

....

How Motors Work

Q1 Complete the passage by choosing from the words below.

force	angle	stronger	magnets	electrons	current	magnetic field	weaker

A wire carrying an electric current in a .... experiences a

.... The bigger the .... and the .... the magnetic field,

the bigger the force. The size of the force also depends on the .... between the

wire and the magnetic field.

Q2 The diagram shows a **conducting wire** between two **magnetic poles**. When the current is switched on, the wire **moves** at right angles to the magnetic field.

a) Draw an arrow on the diagram to show which way the wire moves.

b) How could the wire be made to move in the **opposite** direction?

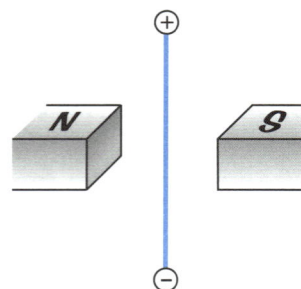

....

Q3 Read the three statements below. Tick the box next to each statement that you think is **true**.

☐ A current-carrying wire will experience a force if it is **parallel** to the magnetic field of a permanent magnet.

☐ A current-carrying wire will experience a force if it is **at right-angles** to the magnetic field of a permanent magnet.

☐ A current-carrying wire will experience a force if it is at an **angle of 45°** to the magnetic field of a permanent magnet.

Q4 The diagram shows a motor that uses a **split-ring commutator**.

a) Tick the box next to each statement that you think is **true**.

☐ The split-ring commutator makes the motor spin faster.

☐ The split-ring commutator reverses the direction of the current every half turn by swapping the contacts to the DC supply.

☐ The split-ring commutator makes the motor rotate in a different direction.

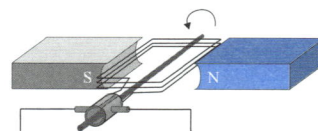

b) Write down two changes you could make to **speed up** the electric motor.

1. ....

2. ....

Power & Efficiency

Q1 Tick the boxes to show whether these statements are **true** or **false**.

True   False

a) The total energy supplied to a machine is called the **total energy input**. ☐ ☐

b) The **useful energy output** of a machine is never more than its total energy input. ☐ ☐

c) The **wasted energy** from a machine is the energy it delivers that's not useful. ☐ ☐

d) The more **efficient** a machine is, the more energy it **wastes**. ☐ ☐

Q2 All machines **waste** some energy.

a) Draw lines to match each machine with its **useful energy change**.

Machines: **Energy changes:**

car   light ⟹ electrical

television   electrical ⟹ light

light bulb   chemical ⟹ kinetic

solar cell   chemical ⟹ electrical

battery   electrical ⟹ light and sound

energy waist ⟹ ENERGY

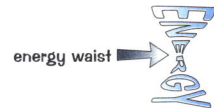

b) In **what form** is energy most **often** wasted?

....

Q3 Fill in the gaps below using the words in the box. Each word can be used once, more than once, or not at all.

| power | current |
| rate | energy | voltage |

Electrical .... is the .... of transfer of electrical ....

The power of an appliance can be calculated using the formula:

power = ... × ....

Q4 Two filament lamps are plugged in to a mains supply of **230 volts**.
Lamp A draws a current of **0.43 amps** and **Lamp B** draws a current of **0.17 amps**.

a) Calculate the power of each lamp.

Lamp A: ....

Lamp B: ....

b) Which lamp is likely to be brighter? ....

c) Which lamp transfers electrical energy into light energy at a greater rate? ....

Energy & Efficiency

Q1 Match up the quantities used for calculating electricity costs with the correct units.

The **power** of an electrical appliance.

The **time** an appliance is used for.

The **price** of electrical energy.

The **electrical energy** used by an appliance.

pence per kilowatt-hour

kilowatt-hour (kWh)

hour (h)

kilowatt (kW)

Q2 All the units in the list below are units of **energy**, except for one.

kilojoule   kilowatt   kilowatt-hour   kWh   J

a) Circle the 'odd one out'.

b) What **is** this a unit of? ....

Q3 The amount of energy an appliance uses depends on its **power** and the **time** it's used for.

a) Calculate how many **kilowatt-hours** of electrical energy a **2 kW** electric heater uses in 3 hours.

Energy used (kWh) = power (kW) × time taken (hours)

= .... × ....

= .... kWh

b) Boris gets his electricity supply from Ivasparkco. They charge 7 pence per kilowatt-hour. Work out the cost of the energy calculated in part a).

Cost of energy = price of one kWh × number of kWh

= .... × ....

= .... pence

Energy & Efficiency

Q4 Match up the beginnings and ends of the sentences below.

Some of the **initial energy input** will ...

... is always the same before and after.

We say energy is "always **conserved**" because the total amount ...

... always be wasted.

Eventually, all the energy supplied to a **machine** ...

... ends up as **heat energy**.

Q5 Trevor pops the kettle on to make a cup of tea. The kettle gets a **total energy input** of **190 kJ**, but only uses **152 kJ** to heat the water.

Efficiency = Useful Energy Output ÷ Total Energy Input

a) How much energy is wasted by the kettle?

....

b) Trevor gets bored waiting for the kettle to boil, so he calculates its efficiency as a percentage. Circle the answer he should get.

92%   **87%**   **78%**   **80%**   **90%**

Q6 Sajid hopes his new MP3 player is better than his old one. He decides to test which one is more **efficient**.

He puts **identical new batteries** in both MP3 players and switches them on. Then he **times** how long they each play for before the batteries run out.

a) Why does Sajid use **new** batteries?

....

b) Write down one thing Sajid must do to make it a **fair test**.

....

c) Player A lasts for 3 hours and Player B lasts for 4 hours. Which Player is the most efficient?

....

Top Tips: Make sure you use the right formulae for energy, cost and energy efficiency. And remember to use the correct units in the cost formula — or you'll get the wrong answer.

Energy Efficiency & Cost-Effectiveness

Q1   Draw arrows to match up the **words** with their **meanings**.

Cost

Cost-effectiveness

Payback time

Effectiveness

How much energy you save.

How much you have to pay.

How long it takes to save as much as you spent initially.

How worthwhile it is to spend the money.

Q2   Heat is lost from a house through its **roof**, **walls**, **doors** and **windows**.

through the roof

....

....

through the walls

....

through the doors

....

....

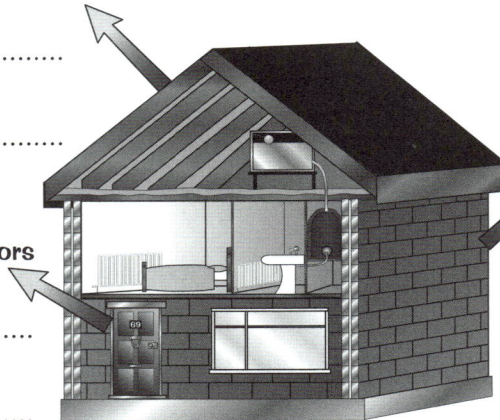

a)   In the spaces on the diagram, write down at least one measure that could be taken to reduce heat losses through each part of the house.

b)   Miss Golightly has just bought a new house which has very large windows.
Suggest three ways she could reduce heat loss through the windows of her new house.

1. ....

2. ....

3. ....

Top Tips: If you want to build a new house, there are regulations about making it energy efficient. If you live in an old house, you can sometimes get a grant to cover the cost of insulation.

Energy Efficiency & Cost-Effectiveness

Q3 Mr Tarantino wants to buy **double glazing** for his house, but the salesman tries to sell him insulated window shutters instead. He says they are cheaper and more **cost-effective**.

	Double glazing	Insulated window shutters
Initial Cost	£3000	£1200
Annual Saving	£60	£20
Payback time	50 years	

a) Calculate the **payback time** for insulated shutters and write it in the table.

b) Is the salesman's advice correct? Give reasons for your answer.

....

....

Q4 Two **washing machines** are on sale with the following labels.

Techno *A-rated*
Power: 2 kW
Average time of cycle: 30 mins
Energy efficiency rating: A
Price: £420

Sudso 2000 *Under £400*
Power: 2 kW
Average time of cycle: 45 mins
Energy efficiency rating: C
Price: £380

a) Calculate the energy consumption (in kWh) for each cycle for a:

i) Techno. ....

ii) Sudso. ....

b) The Adejonwo family does **208 cycles** of washing every **year**.

i) How much **energy** would they save in **one year** by using Techno instead of Sudso?
Give your answer in kilowatt-hours (kWh).

....

....

....

ii) Each year using the Techno would save the family **£8.32**.
What is the **payback time** for the Techno?

Payback time = extra cost ÷ yearly saving.

....

iii) If the Adejonwo family's washing machine lasts 6 years, would it have been **cost-effective** to buy the Techno? Explain your answer.

....

....

Electrical Safety Devices

Q1 Match up the correct colour to each electrical wire.

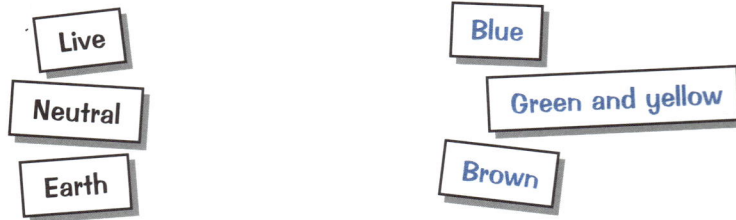

Live

Neutral

Earth

Blue

Green and yellow

Brown

Q2 Circle the correct word(s) from each pair to complete the sentences below.

The live and **neutral** / **earth** wires should normally carry **the same** / **different** current.

Any electrical equipment with a **plastic** / **metal** casing should have the casing connected

to the **earth** / **neutral** wire.

Q3 Put **ticks** in the table to show which wires match each description.

	Live	Neutral	Earth
Must always be connected			
Just for safety			
Electricity normally flows in and out of it			
Alternates between +ve and –ve voltage			

Morris thought it best to be earthed at all times — just in case.

Q4 Tick the boxes to show whether these statements are **true** or **false**.

True False

a) The **earth** wire in an electrical cable carries the same current as the **live** and **neutral** wires. ☐ ☐

b) **Neutral** wires are often connected to cold water pipes in the home. ☐ ☐

c) Fuses are placed in the **live** wire of the cable. ☐ ☐

Q5 These sentences describe how a **fuse** and **earth wire** work together to prevent you getting an electric shock from a toaster. Put numbers in the table to show the order they should go in.

	The surge in current causes the fuse wire to heat up.
	Everything is now safe.
1	A fault develops and the earthed casing becomes connected to the live supply.
	The live supply is cut off.
	The fuse melts.
	A large current now flows in through the live wire and out through the earth wire.

Energy from New Technology

Q1   Tick the boxes to show whether these statements are **true** or **false**.

		True	False
a)	Biomass can only be obtained from dead animals and plants.	☐	☐
b)	Solar panels can only work where it is constantly sunny.	☐	☐
c)	Tidal barrages could affect fish migration.	☐	☐
d)	Renewables cause less pollution than fossil fuels.	☐	☐
e)	Wind turbines can only be sited on hilltops.	☐	☐

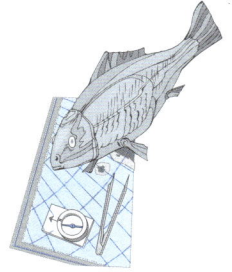

Q2   On a sunny day, a **solar panel** receives **1.5 kW** of power from the Sun. The panel is **15% efficient**.

a)   How much power does the solar panel generate?

....

b)   On a cloudy day the sunlight on the panel could drop to **0.5 kW**.
How much power would the solar panel generate in this weather?

....

c)   Calculate how many of these panels would be needed to power a **4.5 kW** motor:

i)   on a sunny day.

....

ii)   on a cloudy day.

....

Q3   Only a small amount of the UK's energy comes from **solar** and other **renewable** energy resources.

a)   Give two advantages of renewable energy resources compared to non-renewable resources.

1. ....

2. ....

b)   Give one reason why people may **not want** to use solar panels.

....

c)   Why are solar panels a better energy resource in **Southern Italy** than they are in **Southern Ireland**?

....

Top Tips: New technology could be our saviour — if it can help us meet our energy needs without trashing the planet. It might help if we reduce the amount of energy we **use**, too.

Energy from New Technology

Q4 People often **object** to **wind turbines** being put up near to where they live.

a) Give two reasons why they might **object**.

....

....

....

b) List three arguments **in favour** of using wind turbines to generate electricity.

1. ....

2. ....

3. ....

Q5 Choose the **best renewable** option from the list below for each of the given **situations**.
Give a **reason** for each choice that you make.

Renewable options: geothermal, biomass, wave converters, wind turbines, hydroelectric.

a) Situation 1: a small **flat** island in the middle of an ocean, with **little wind** and a **low rainfall**.

Choice .... Reason ....

....

b) Situation 2: a **hilly** area with **low rainfall**.

Choice .... Reason ....

....

c) Situation 3: a **hilly** area with **high rainfall**.

Choice .... Reason ....

....

d) Situation 4: an area with **hot water geysers**.

Choice .... Reason ....

....

Mixed Questions — P1a Topics 9 & 10

Q1 Dr Fergals has developed a new type of **insulation**, material X, for insulating **hot water tanks**.

a) Fill in the blanks to complete the description below of how Dr Fergals could compare the **effectiveness** of material X and fibreglass wool. You may need to use some words more than once.

any	the same	identical	different	more	energy	less

Insulate two .... hot water tanks, one with material X and the

other with fibreglass wool. Heat the water in both tanks to ....

temperature(s), then measure how much .... it takes to maintain

that temperature for seven days. The tank which needs .... energy

to maintain its temperature must have .... effective insulation.

b) Dr Fergals decides to compare the **cost-effectiveness** of his new material and fibreglass wool.

i) Complete the table below. Electricity costs **14 pence per kWh**.

Type of lagging	Energy used in 1 week (kWh)	Cost per year (£)	Saving per year (£)	Initial cost (£)	Payback time (years)
None	10		-	0	-
Fibreglass wool	8			60	
Material X	6			100	

ii) Which material is more cost-effective? ....

Q2 The diagram shows a **generator** that is turned by a wind turbine.

a) Give one advantage and one disadvantage of using wind power to generate all the UK's electricity.

Advantage: ....

Disadvantage: ....

....

turned by wind turbine

magnet

N   S

soft iron

coil

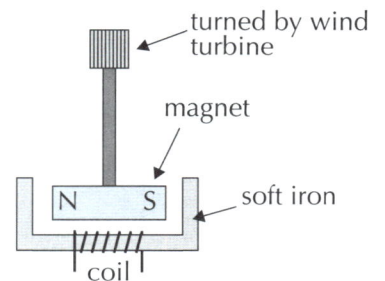

b) Give two other examples of renewable resources that can be used to generate electricity.

1. ....   2. ....

c) The generator is attached to a cathode ray oscilloscope (CRO).

i) Circle the letter of the diagram that could show the output of the generator.

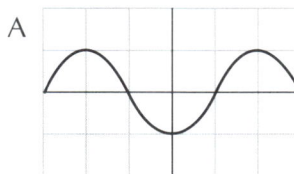

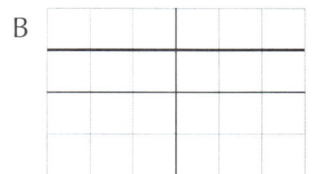

A

B

ii) Suggest a source for the other diagram.

....

iii) How would the CRO trace change if the magnet was rotated **twice as fast**?

....

Mixed Questions — P1a Topics 9 & 10

Q3 When Mike goes potholing, he wears a **torch** on his helmet so he can see where he is going.

Mike normally uses a **3 V** dry-cell battery with a stated capacity of **20 A h**.

a) For how long can it supply a current of **250 mA**?

....

b) Mike uses five batteries with different voltage ratings to investigate his torch's **bulb**.

i) State the equation relating current, voltage and resistance.

....

ii) The graph shows Mike's results. Why have the results produced a **curved** graph?

....

....

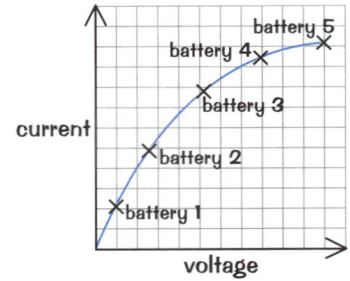

c) Pete, Mike's friend, powers his torch with a battery that he charges with a **solar cell**. Pete uses a datalogger to record the amount of sunlight available while the battery charges.

Give one advantage of using a **datalogging** system to record data.

....

d) After charging the battery, Pete switches his torch on. The bulb goes off after **1980 s**. The power rating of Pete's torch is 0.3 W. Complete the table to calculate the combined efficiency of the torch and solar cell.

Energy input	Useful energy output	Efficiency
4200 J		

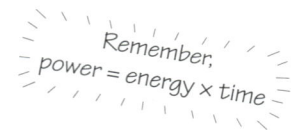

*Remember,
power = energy × time*

Q4 The diagram below shows a simple **motor** from a hairdryer. The coil is rotating as shown.

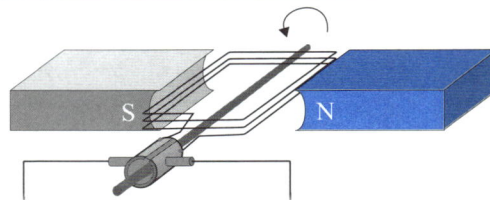

a) Use Fleming's Left-Hand Rule to work out which way the current flows on each arm of the coil, then draw arrows labelled 'I' on the diagram to indicate the directions.

The electricity supply is at **230 V** and the power rating of the hairdryer is **350 W**.

b) i) What is meant by 'electrical power'? ....

ii) Calculate the current the hairdryer draws. ....

c) The **temperature** of the air coming from the hairdryer must be kept within certain limits. What component could be used to automatically control the heater in the hairdryer?

....

Use of Waves in Scanning

Q1 Circle the correct word(s) from each pair to complete this passage.

X-rays can pass easily through soft tissue / bones but are reflected / absorbed more by bones / skin. Screens and shields made of plastic / lead are used to minimise unnecessary exposure to X-rays.

Q2 **Draw lines** to match the waves to their **uses**.

microwaves

X-rays

ultraviolet

visible

to detect forged bank notes

to measure cloud patterns

to examine X-ray photographs

to detect fractures in bones

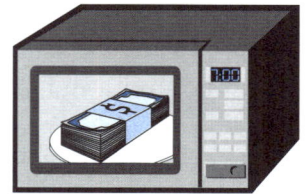

Q3 Use the words in the box to **complete the paragraph** about **infrared** radiation.

| bright | dark | electrical | black | heat |
| audible | hot | night-vision | daytime | |

Infrared is another name for .... radiation.

People give out infrared because they are ....

The police use .... equipment to let them see

people in the .... The equipment changes

infrared into an .... signal which then appears

as a .... spot on a screen.

Q4 Tick the boxes to show whether the following statements are **true** or **false**.

		True	False
a)	X-ray photographs show "shadows of our bones".	☐	☐
b)	Flesh is more dense than bone so it lets X-rays through more easily.	☐	☐
c)	Radiographers wear lead aprons to protect their clothing.	☐	☐
d)	X-rays don't easily pass through bones because they are absorbed by them.	☐	☐

Use of Waves in Scanning

Q5   Which of the following works by wave **reflection**? Circle the correct boxes.

reading a book   night-vision camera

prenatal scanning   X-rays

Q6   For each of these questions on **iris scanning**, tick the appropriate box.

a)   How is **iris data** obtained?

☐ It is entered into a computer.

☐ It is translated into a code.

☐ It is photographed with a camera.

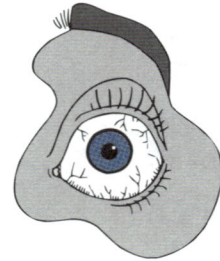

b)   What makes iris data good for **security checks**?

☐ Everybody has a unique pattern.

☐ It works in low-intensity light.

☐ It is totally foolproof.

Q7   Complete the passage by choosing from the words below.

sex	normally	X-rays	lasers	slow
Down's syndrome	influenza	ultrasound	dangerous	abortion

Prenatal scanning uses .... to make a video image of a

developing foetus. You could also do a scan using .... but it

would be more .... Parents might want a prenatal scan to check

the foetus is developing ...., find its .... and

check for .... This might present hard choices about whether or

not to have an ....

Top Tips: It's not enough just to know how ultrasound scanning can be used to produce images of a foetus — you also need to consider the ethical issues involved. It's a good idea to have a think about these now so that you'll know what the arguments are when it comes to the exam.

Use of Waves in Scanning

Q8 **Ultraviolet radiation** is useful in detecting bank note forgeries.

a) Tick the boxes to show whether these statements are **true** or **false**.

True False

i) Fluorescent materials reflect ultraviolet radiation. ☐ ☐

ii) Fluorescent materials emit visible light. ☐ ☐

iii) Under a UV light, fake bank notes often emit no radiation. ☐ ☐

b) Explain how banks can detect forgeries using **fluorescent ink** on their banknotes.

....

....

....

Q9 This diagram represents a **rainfall radar** picture of part of Britain.

a) Underline the correct sentence.

Rainfall is detected using microwaves emitted from space.

Rainfall is detected using ultraviolet radiation.

Rainfall is detected using microwaves emitted from transmitters on the ground.

Cromer, Thorpe Market, King's Lynn, Norwich, Great Yarmouth, Lowestoft

b) What happens to the waves that are **not reflected back** to make the picture?

....

c) i) In which of the places shown is it likely to have been **raining** when the picture was taken?

....

ii) How can you tell?

....

Top Tips: As I'm sure you well know there are loads of different practical uses of waves. Make sure you know these uses and any limitations they have — it could just pop up on the exam.

Waves — Basic Principles

Q1 A sumo wrestler jumps into a canal, sending waves across to the other side. A wave arrives **once every second**. The distance between their peaks is **0.2 m**.

$v = f\lambda$

a) What is the **frequency** of the waves? ....

b) Use the **wave equation** to calculate the **speed** of the waves. ....

Q2 Diagrams A, B and C represent **electromagnetic waves**.

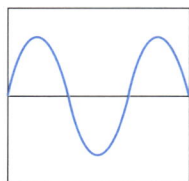 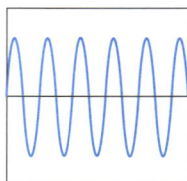 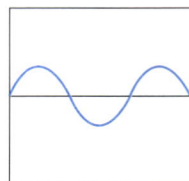

A   **B**   **C**

a) Which two diagrams show waves with the same **frequency**? ...... and ......

b) Which two diagrams show waves with the same **amplitude**? ...... and ......

c) Which two diagrams show waves with the same **wavelength**? ...... and ......

Q3 A ripple in a pond travels at **0.5 m/s**. It makes a duck bob up and down **twice every second**.

a) What is the **frequency** of the duck's bobbing? ....

Remember what's meant by a wavelength, then rearrange $v = f\lambda$.

b) When the duck is on the crest of a wave, **how far away** is the next crest?

....

Q4 The graph is a **CRO** representation of a **sound wave**.

a) What is the **amplitude** of the wave on the CRO screen?

....

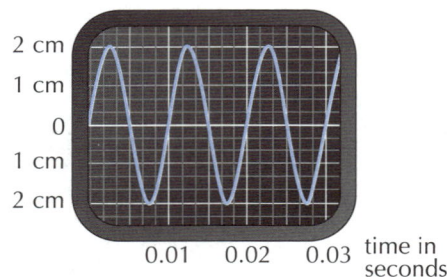

b) How much **time** does a full wave take to pass? ....

Q5 Change the frequencies below into **hertz** and **standard form**.

90 MHz   900 kHz   9 000 000 Hz 9×10^2 MHz

....

More Waves — Principles

Q1 Here are **two ways** in which you can make waves on a **slinky** spring.

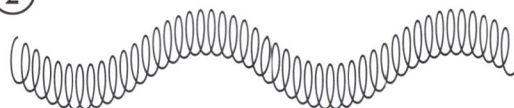

Which diagram shows a **transverse** wave, and which one shows a **longitudinal** wave?

Transverse: ....   Longitudinal: ....

Q2 Sort the waves below into two groups — **longitudinal** waves and **transverse** waves.

sunlight   'push-pull' wave on a slinky   ultraviolet   'shake' wave on a slinky

ultrasound   microwaves   birdsong   drumbeat

Longitudinal: ....

Transverse: ....

Q3 Sound waves are **longitudinal** waves.

a) Indicate whether these sentences are true or false:

		True	False
i)	Vibrations in a longitudinal wave are at 90° to the direction the wave is travelling.	☐	☐
ii)	Light is an example of a longitudinal wave.	☐	☐
iii)	CRO displays always show longitudinal waves as transverse waves.	☐	☐

b) As sound waves travel through a material they produce **compressions** and **rarefactions**. Label these on the diagram below.

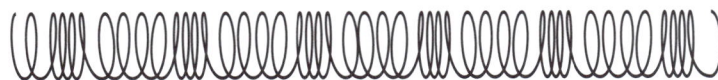

Q4 Circle the letters to show which of the following statements about waves are **true**.

A Absorption of waves can increase the temperature of objects.

B Transverse waves are all electromagnetic.

C Longitudinal waves cannot be displayed on a CRO.

D A compression happens when the medium is squashed.

Reflection of Waves

Q1 The diagram shows a sound wave travelling down a corridor, **bouncing** off a wall, and then being heard by a man. It takes the sound **0.5 seconds** to reach him. Calculate the **speed** of the sound wave.

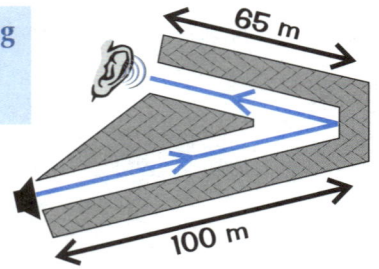

....

....

Use speed = distance / time

65 m

100 m

Q2 Use these words to complete the passage.

boundary	density	images	medium	reflected	incidence

When a wave goes from one .... to another, some of

its energy is .... at the .... between

them. This allows us to see .... in transparent objects.

This partial reflection can be caused by changes in ....

The angle of reflection is the same as the angle of ....

Q3 A boat is sending pulses of **ultrasound** down to the seabed and then receiving the reflection. The sea is **750 m deep** where the boat is, and it takes **1 second** to receive the echo.

a) How **fast** does the ultrasound travel in the sea water?

....

b) If the boat passes over a **wreck**, what will happen to the time taken to receive the echo?

....

Q4 A boy stands **165 m** away from the wall of a football stadium. He claps his hands and listens for the echo. When he claps **once every second**, each **echo** coincides with the **next clap**.

a) **i)** Calculate the distance travelled by the wave before he hears the echo.

....

ii) Calculate the speed of sound from this experiment.

....

b) Underline the correct sentence(s).

If he moves further from the wall, the speed of the sound increases.

If he claps harder, the echo will come back to him sooner.

If he moves away from the wall, it takes longer for the echo to get back to him.

Refraction of Waves

Q1 Diagrams A and B show waves travelling from a **less dense** medium to a **denser** medium.

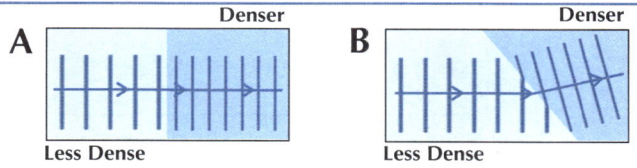

A Denser / Less Dense

B Denser / Less Dense

a) Which diagram shows the waves being **refracted**? ....

b) Why does refraction **not happen** in the other diagram?

....

c) What happens to the **velocity** of the waves as they pass into the denser medium?

....

Q2 Jo is looking at a pebble lying on the bottom of a **pool**. Circle the correct words to complete the sentences.

a) The bottom of the pool appears to be **nearer to** / **further from** Jo than it actually is.

b) Water is **less** / **more** dense than air.

c) Light travels **faster** / **slower** in air than in water.

Q3 The diagram shows a light ray passing through **air** and **glass**.

a) Fill in the gaps below to say which medium is **air** and which is **glass**.

Medium 1 is ....

Medium 2 is ....

medium 1

medium 2

b) **Explain** your answer to part a).

....

....

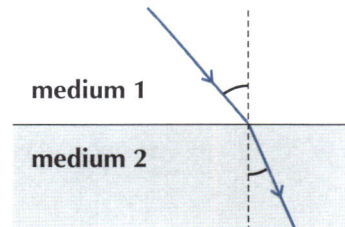

c) Would your answer to a) be the **same** if the wave was a **sound wave**? Explain why.

....

Q4 The diagram below shows rays of light entering two **glass prisms**.
For each prism **sketch the path** the ray would take as it passed through the prism.

It helps to sketch in the normal to each boundary. Then you can see more clearly whether the ray is refracted towards it or away.

Electromagnetic Waves

Q1   Complete the following sentences by circling the correct word(s) from each pair.

> All electromagnetic waves transfer matter / energy from place to place.
>
> In a vacuum they travel at the same speed / different speeds.

Q2   Tick the boxes to show whether the following statements are **true** or **false**.

		True	False
a)	Visible light travels faster in a vacuum than both X-rays and radio waves.	☐	☐
b)	EM waves with higher frequencies have longer wavelengths.	☐	☐
c)	Radio waves have the shortest wavelength of all EM waves.	☐	☐
d)	All EM waves can travel through space.	☐	☐

Q3   **Red** and **violet** are at opposite ends of the spectrum of **visible** light. Draw lines to attach each statement to one or both of them.

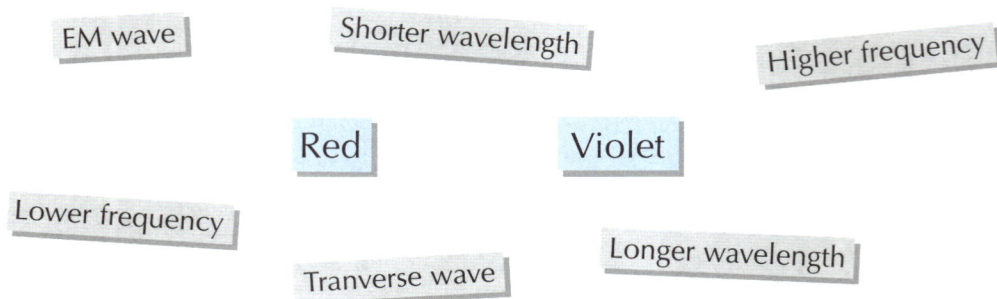

EM wave   Shorter wavelength   Higher frequency

Red   Violet

Lower frequency   Longer wavelength

Tranverse wave

Q4   The graph opposite shows how the **energy** of EM waves varies with **frequency**.

a)   What is the relationship between frequency and energy?

....

....

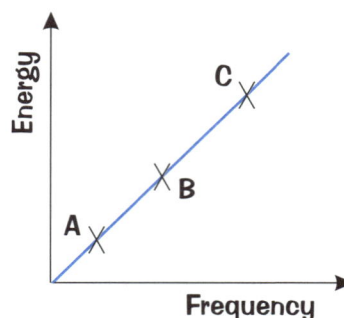

b)   Draw **arrows** to match points **A**, **B** and **C** from the graph to the **three types of radiation** below.

green light	gamma radiation	radio waves
A	B	C

Electromagnetic Waves

Q5 Fill in the blanks using the words in blue.

> overexposure   UV rays   ionising   dark   liver   skin
> sunscreen   X-rays   mutations   pale   explode

Excessive sunbathing can be dangerous because sunlight contains

.........................., some of which are .... They

can cause cell ...., which can lead to

.... cancer. Skin is better protected if it is

.... because it stops more radiation reaching the

tissue below. You should always avoid .... to the

sun and use .... when outside for a long time.

Q6 Here are four different types of **electromagnetic wave**:

> ultraviolet   microwaves   X-rays   infrared

a) Which has the **lowest frequency**? ....

b) Which carries the **most energy**? ....

c) Which can cause damage by **ionisation**? ....

Q7 Some EM radiation can be **harmful** to the body.

a) Match each type of EM radiation to the damage it can cause to the human body.

Microwaves   mutation or destruction of cells

Infrared   heating of body tissue

X-rays   skin burns

b) **i)** What type of waves do mobile phones use? ....

ii) Why are some people concerned about the increasing use of mobile phones?

....

....

Top Tips: Scientists have to weigh up evidence when deciding how risky an activity is — and the more evidence they have, the more confident they can be in their predictions. We already know enough about EM waves in general to be able to say which ones cause the most damage to the body.

<u>*Digital Technology*</u>

Q1 Draw lines to match the labels to the diagrams below.

a 'noisy' digital signal   a 'noisy' analogue signal   a 'clean' digital signal

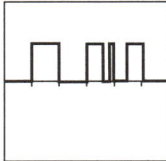   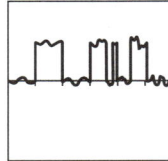   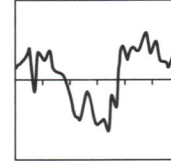

Q2 **Fill in the blanks**, using the words below.

analogue	digital	amplified	weaken	interference	noise

All signals .... as they travel. To overcome this, they can be

.... Signals may also suffer .... from

other signals or from electrical disturbances. This causes ....

in the signal. When .... signals are amplified, the noise is

also amplified.

Q3 Signals can either be **analogue** or **digital**, and both can pick up noise as they travel.

a) Digital signals suffer less from **noise** than analogue signals. Circle the correct words in this passage.

A digital signal contains many / two values, which are normally referred to as

0 and 1 / 50 and 100. If a digital signal is noisy, it's usually easy / hard to tell what the

original signal looked like, so noise is more / less of a problem than with analogue signals.

b) State one other **advantage** of using digital signals for communication.

....

Q4 Digital technology has had a big impact on the **music industry**.

a) Give **two** examples of ways in which digital technology has changed the way music is **stored**.

1. ....

2. ....

b) Give an example of a new sort of **musical instrument** that has been produced as a result of digital technology.

....

Digital Technology

Q5   Choose from the words below to complete the passage.

pulses	thousands	reflected	internal	diffraction	dense	core	infrared	gamma

Optical fibres depend on total .... reflection for their operation. Visible

light or .... waves are sent down the cable and are ....

when they hit the boundary between the .... and the less

.... outer layer. The signals travel as .... of radiation.

Each cable can carry .... of different signals.

Q6   Doctors can use an **endoscope** to look inside a patient's body. An endoscope has two bundles of **optical fibres** — one carries light down into your stomach, say, and the other returns the reflected light back to a monitor.

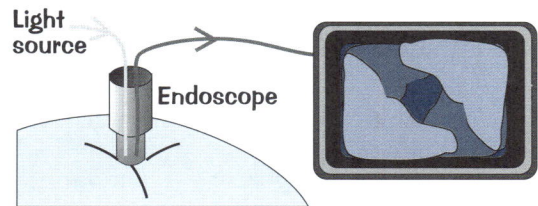

Light source

Endoscope

a)   Optical fibres work because of **total internal reflection** within the fibre. If there **wasn't** total internal reflection inside the fibre, **what would happen** to the signal sent down the fibre?

....

b)   On this diagram, draw lines to show the path that a ray transmitting a signal could take.

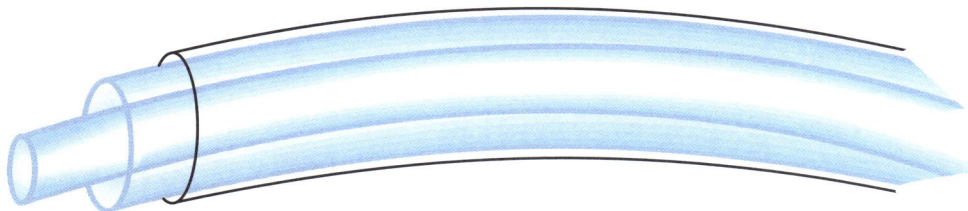

Q7   Old-fashioned dial-up internet connections use **copper wires**. **Optical fibres** are used for broadband connections. Give two **advantages** of using optical fibres instead of copper wires.

1. ....

2. ....

> ## Top Tips: Luckily you **don't** need to know the **gory details** of how total internal reflection works for this module. You just need to know that it happens, and what **optical fibres** are used for.

The Solar System

Q1 Choose from the words in the box to **complete the paragraph**.

asteroid belt	inner	Saturn	Jupiter	Mars	moons	Solar System	asteroid

The .... is made up of the Sun and its surrounding

planets. The four planets closest to the Sun are known as the ....

planets while the rest of the planets are called the outer planets. Between these two

types of planet there is also an ....

Some of the planets are orbited by natural satellites called ....

Q2 Even though the Earth's radius is a massive 6378 km, it's very small compared to the scale of the Universe.

a) Rearrange the following list of **astronomical things** into size order, starting with the smallest.

galaxy   moon   star   planet   Universe

.... ➡ .... ➡ .... ➡ .... ➡ ....

b) Fill in the table of **astronomical distances** with the **numbers 1-4**, to put them into the **correct order of size**. Make the smallest distance number 1 and the largest distance number 4.

	Distance between Earth and Sun
	Distance between stars
	Distance between galaxies
	Distance between Earth and Moon

Q3 Which one of the following statements is **not true**? Tick the appropriate box.

☐ A galaxy is made up of millions (or even billions) of stars.

☐ The distance between galaxies can be millions of times the distance between stars.

☐ Gravity is the force which keeps stars apart.

☐ Galaxies rotate in space.

The Solar System

Q4 Draw lines to join up each **central box** with correct descriptions from the boxes on the right and left.

Some boxes might have more than one line going to them...

They are usually smaller than planets.

Billions of these make up the Milky Way.

They give out light and heat.

STARS

PLANETS

MOONS

They can be seen because of reflected light.

They orbit planets.

They orbit stars.

Q5 Indicate whether each of these statements is **true** or **false**.

True False

a) Mercury is the nearest planet to the Sun. ☐ ☐

b) Planets orbit the Sun in perfect circular orbits. ☐ ☐

c) The stars in galaxies move as the galaxy slowly rotates. ☐ ☐

d) The Sun is at the centre of the Milky Way galaxy. ☐ ☐

Q6 A typical modern explorer spacecraft can travel at **17 kilometres a second**.

a) Use this information to complete the table below.

	Distance from Earth / km	Time for an explorer craft to reach here / seconds
Jupiter	630 000 000	
Our nearest star (beyond the Sun)	39 900 000 000 000	

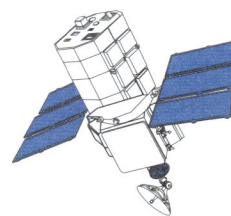

Remember — time = distance ÷ speed

b) Approximately how many **years** would it take to reach our nearest star (beyond the Sun)?

....

c) Why would it be **difficult to communicate** with a spacecraft halfway to Jupiter?

....

....

The Universe

Q1   Read the following passage and **underline the correct word or words** in each pair.

Comets are balls of ice and dust that orbit the Sun in circular / **elongated elliptical** orbits. They often orbit in **the same plane as** / **a different plane from** the planets. When comets approach the Sun they **speed up** / **slow down** because the Sun's gravity has **more** / **less** of an effect. If a comet passes close to Earth's orbit it is known as a Near Earth Object, or NEO.

Q2   Almost all asteroids in the Solar System lie in the **asteroid belt**.

a)   Between which two planets would you find the asteroid belt?

.... and ....

b)   What might cause an asteroid to **leave its orbit** and head **towards Earth**?

....

c)   Write down two ways in which the orbit of a **comet** is different from the orbit of an **asteroid**.

1. ....

2. ....

Q3   Tick the correct box to show whether each of these statements is **true** or **false**.   True   False

a)   The Sun is at the centre of a comet's orbit.   ☐   ☐

b)   Occasionally a meteor will cause damage on Earth.   ☐   ☐

c)   The Universe is mostly empty space.   ☐   ☐

d)   A comet hitting the Earth could cause earthquakes.   ☐   ☐

Q4   Astronomers track the trajectories of **NEOs**.

a)   Apart from comets, name one type of astronomical object that could be an NEO.

....

b)   Explain why we should be worried if an NEO was found on a collision course with Earth.

....

....

Hint — what may have happened to the dinosaurs?

Space Flight

Q1 Which of the following disorders is not recognised as a potential problem on a long space flight? Circle the correct letter **A-D**.

    A Wasted muscles   **B** Weak bones

    C Bruising   **D** Psychological problems

Q2 It would be a **very bad idea** to go out into **space** without any **protection**.

a) Write down one **hazard** associated with **exposure** to the **Sun's rays**.

....

b) Why are space suits **pressurised**?

....

c) Give one other problem an astronaut would face in space without proper protection.

....

Q3 Match up the following **effects of space flight** with the **on-board solutions** designed to minimise them.

weak muscles   radiation shields

skin cancer   special diet

bone wastage   special exercises

Q4 Long space missions carry a **higher risk** to the astronauts' health than shorter space missions.

a) Why would the Sun's radiation cause **more** problems on a mission to **Mars** than one to the **Moon**?

....

b) Why are long space missions bad for the **heart**?

....

....

c) Give one reason why space flight can cause **mental stress** (as well as physical problems).

....

Forces and Space Flight

Q1   Newton's force laws apply in space as well as on Earth.

a)   Fill in the gaps in this statement about forces:

Each action has an .... and .... reaction.

b)   A spacecraft's **rocket engine** burns fuel, producing exhaust gas.
Underline the correct word in each pair to explain how this makes the spacecraft **accelerate**.

> The exhaust gas is pushed out of the front / back of the spacecraft by the
> action / reaction force. The spacecraft has a(n) equal / double reaction force
> pushing it forwards / backwards.

Q2   Jean Luc has landed his rocket safely on the surface of the Moon.
On the Moon, his rocket weighs **48 200 N**.

a)   What force stops the rocket sinking into the ground?

....

b)   Write down the size of this force.

....

Q3   Circle any of the situations below in which there is an **acceleration**.

A car slowing down.   **Jane playing on a swing.**

A planet orbiting a star.   **A tractor travelling at a constant
speed on a straight level road.**

Q4   Karl throws a **750 g** pie at Susan, giving it an acceleration of **3.8 m/s²**.

a)   Write down the equation that links acceleration, force and mass.

....

b)   Calculate the force of Karl's throw.

....

Forces and Space Flight

Q5 Two spacecraft have been fitted with the **same rocket engine**. The first has a mass of 1100 kg and an acceleration of 28.0 m/s². The second only manages an acceleration of 19.25 m/s².

a) Calculate the **force** the engine can exert.

....

b) What's the **mass** of the second spacecraft, to the nearest kg? Circle the correct answer.

1440 kg   1500 kg   1730 kg   1600 kg

Q6 A spacecraft launches a probe at a **constant speed**. A day later, the probe returns from the same direction at the **same speed**. Circle the letter(s) next to any **true** statements below.

A The probe returned at the same speed and so **must** have burned some fuel.

B The probe returned at a different velocity and so **must not** have burnt any fuel.

C The probe returned with a different velocity and so it must have **accelerated** at some point on its journey.

Q7 A **5000 kg** spacecraft is going to land on a planet. It **accelerates** towards the planet, then as it approaches the planet's surface it **slows right down** for a gentle landing.

a) The spacecraft accelerates at **10 m/s²**. Calculate the force acting on the spacecraft.

....

b) Assuming the planet's atmosphere is thin, is it enough for the spacecraft to **switch off** its rocket engine in order to **slow down**? **Explain** your answer.

If the atmosphere is thin assume there's no friction or air resistance.

....

....

c) If the atmosphere was thicker, would the rocket slow down more or less quickly? Explain your answer.

....

Top Tips: There are **two important things to learn** if you want to get these questions right. The first one is the rule about **action** and **reaction**. The second one's about **F**, **m** and **a**...

Gravity, Mass and Weight

Q1   Which of these statements about **gravity** are **true**? Circle the appropriate letters.

    A   Gravity is an attractive force between the weights of two objects.

    B   Gravity is the force that keeps the Moon orbiting the Earth.

    C   Objects have mass because of gravity.

    D   The bigger the mass, the stronger its gravity is.

Q2   Match the beginning and end of each sentence below.

Mass is ...

Weight is caused by ...

Mass is not a ...

Weight is measured in ...

... newtons.

... force.

... the pull of gravity.

... the amount of 'stuff' in an object.

Q3   Two scientists are discussing a trip to **Mars**. They have different points of view.

Professor Brown: "We need less fuel for the return trip — the rocket has less mass on Mars."
Professor White: "We need less fuel for the return trip because the rocket weighs less on Mars."

Who is right, and why is the other wrong? (Ignore the amount of fuel burned getting to Mars.)

....

....

Q4   Gillian is sick of diets but wants to lose some weight. She has a mass of **90 kg**.

a)   How much does she **weigh** on Earth? (Assume g = 10 m/s^2.)

....

b)   She packs her cream cakes and decides to go to the planet Lardas.
If **g = 12.6 m/s^2** on this planet, calculate her weight on this planet.

....

c)   She decides to catch the shuttle to Choco 7, where she only weighs **702 N**.
Work out the strength of gravity, **g**, for this planet.

....

The Life Cycle of Stars

Q1   Complete the passage, choosing from the words given below.

gravity	millions	hot	fusion	stable	inwards
outwards		billions		fission	mass

When a protostar gets .... enough, hydrogen nuclei start to

undergo nuclear .... and the star enters its ....

phase (becoming a main sequence star). The force from the heat generated

inside the star (pushing ....) and the force of gravity (pushing

...............................) are balanced. The star might stay in this stable phase for

.... of years.

Q2   Towards the end of its life, a **main sequence** star will become a **red giant**.

a)   What causes a star to become a **red giant**?

....

....

b)   Why is a red giant **red**?

....

c)   What will small stars like our Sun eventually become? Circle the letter next to the correct answer.

A   White Dwarf   **B**   Black Hole   **C**   Neutron Star

Q3   Complete the following passage by circling the correct word(s) from each pair.

When a star starts to run out of hydrogen, it becomes a
red **dwarf** / **giant**. Large stars eventually explode,
throwing out layers of dust and gas into space, leaving
behind a **light** / **dense** core. This explosion is called a **big**
bang / **supernova**. The core becomes either a **neutron** /
proton star or a **white dwarf** / **black hole**.

The Life Cycle of Stars

Q4   Below is a diagram showing the **life cycle** of **stars**.

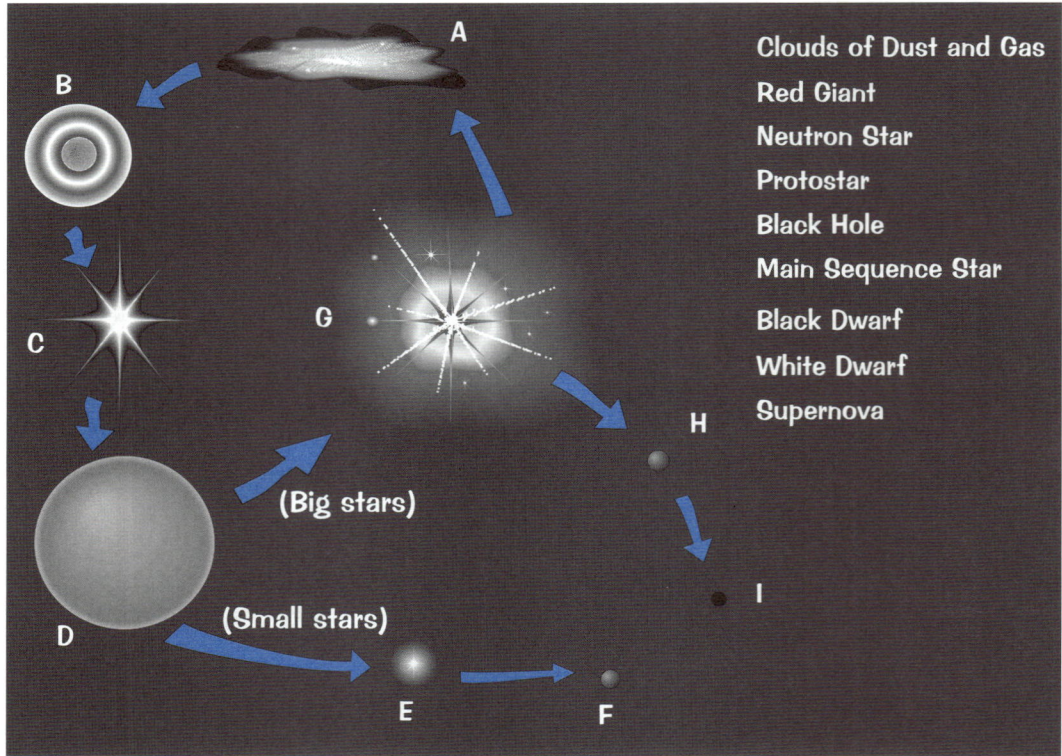

Clouds of Dust and Gas
Red Giant
Neutron Star
Protostar
Black Hole
Main Sequence Star
Black Dwarf
White Dwarf
Supernova

Match the letters to the words on the right of the diagram.

A ....

B ....

C ....

D ....

E ....

F ....

G ....

H ....

I ....

Q5   Explain how scientists can tell the Sun is a **second generation star** by looking at the chemical elements that make up Earth.

Hint — where and when are heavy elements made?

....

....

....

Top Tips: This star life cycle might seem a bit weird and wonderful, but really it's just a **series of events** that you've got to **learn**.   If you don't remember which things happen to big stars and which happen to smaller stars (like our Sun) get your books and notes out and **revise** it.

Robots and Remote Sensing

Q1 Scientists use **remote sensing** to investigate other planets.

a) Which one of the following is a robot lander that has investigated the surface of **Mars**? Circle the correct answer.

  Norman   Viking   Saxon

b) Give an advantage of **remote sensing**, compared to landing a robot on the surface of a planet.

....

....

c) Give an advantage of **landing a robot** on the **surface** of a planet, compared to remote sensing.

....

....

d) Give one example of data that scientists could collect using remote sensing.

....

Q2 The diagram shows a (made-up) **space probe** called **Erik** orbiting **Titan**, which is one of **Saturn's moons**.

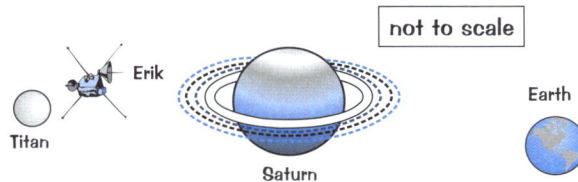

not to scale

Erik · Titan · Saturn · Earth

a) How would Erik **transmit data** back to Earth?

....

b) i) When Erik is in the position shown in the diagram, it **can't transmit data** to Earth. Why not?

....

ii) How could scientists **get around** this problem?

....

Hint — what could Erik be programmed to do until it's in a better position?

....

Is There Anybody Out There?

Q1   Tick the correct box to show whether the following statements are **true** or **false**.   **True**   **False**

a)   Scientists have detected other planets outside our Solar System.   ☐ ☐

b)   Evidence of intelligent life has been found on other planets in our Solar System.   ☐ ☐

c)   There are probably very few Earth-like planets capable of supporting life in our galaxy.   ☐ ☐

Q2   The **SETI** project search for narrow band radio signals from space.

a)   What does **SETI** stand for? Circle the correct answer.

Scientific Extra Terrestrial Investigation.

Search for Extra Terrestrial intelligence.

Scientific Exploration into Terrestrial Intelligence.

b)   Write down one object in space that adds to the radio **noise** detected.

....

We're HERE!   Over 'ere lads

THIS WAY

c)   How can the **general public** help SETI with this?

....

....

d)   Write down one other type of signal SETI are now looking for.

....

Q3   Susan says that if **intelligent life** really existed outside Earth, we would have been **contacted** by aliens **before now** — and we **haven't** been contacted, therefore we are **alone** in the Universe.

Give two reasons why Susan could be wrong.

1. ....

2. ....

Top Tips:
So... is there anyone out there? The quick and simple answer is — we don't know. It would just be a bit too weird if in the whole great big enormous Universe our little planet was the only thing with life on it. There must be **something** out there (surely)... but we've just not found it yet.

The Origins of the Universe

Q1 The **Big Bang** theory is the generally accepted scientific explanation for the origin of the Universe.

a) Complete this passage using the words supplied:

expansion	matter	energy	expand	age	explosion

Many scientists believe that the Universe started with all the ....

and .... in one small space. There was a huge

.... and the Universe started to ....

b) The Big Bang caused the Universe to **expand**. What is the Universe doing now?
Circle the correct answer.

　　　　it's contracting　　　　　　　it's expanding　　　　　　　neither

Q2 The **galaxies in an expanding universe** can be likened to
particles on the surface of a **bubble** which is **getting bigger**.

a) What happens to two "particles" which start off **next** to each other as the bubble **expands**?

　　..

b) Astronomers can tell how fast the Universe is expanding by looking at the motions of the galaxies.
Why do astronomers want to know the speed of the Universe's expansion?

　　..

c) If there was no gravity, what would happen to the expansion rate of the Universe?

　　..

Q3 The '**Big Bang**' and '**Steady State**' theories are two theories of the origin of the Universe.

a) Briefly explain the idea behind the Steady State theory.

　　..

　　..

b) How does this theory explain the expansion of the Universe?
Tick the box next to the correct answer.

　　☐　　It can't explain it. It is one of the problems with the theory.

　　☐　　It states that the Universe isn't expanding — it's an optical illusion.

　　☐　　It suggests that matter is being created as the Universe expands.

The Future of the Universe

Q1 The Oscillating Universe theory is one theory that predicts how the Universe began and will end. Circle the letter next to the true statement below.

A The Oscillating Universe theory states that the Universe is in an endless cycle of contraction and expansion.

B The Oscillating Universe theory states that the Universe will expand forever.

C The Oscillating Universe theory states that the Universe will completely end in a Big Crunch.

Q2 In the future the Universe will do one of two things.

a) Write down the two possible fates of the Universe.

1. ....

2. ....

b) Write down the two factors that the fate of the Universe depends on.

1. ....

2. ....

Q3 **Number** these statements to show the **order of events** in the **Oscillating Universe theory**. The first one has been done for you.

☐ Gravity stops the Universe expanding.

☐ The next Big Bang happens.

☐ The Universe expands.

☐ All matter is compressed to a point.

☐ 1 The Big Bang happens.

☐ Gravity starts to make the Universe contract.

Your life line is very long...

Q4 Tick the correct box to show whether each of these statements is **true** or **false**.

		True	False
a)	We can measure approximately how fast the Universe is expanding.	☐	☐
b)	The Universe will definitely end in a Big Crunch.	☐	☐
c)	There are no unsolved problems in astrophysics.	☐	☐

Mixed Questions — P1b Topics 11 & 12

Q1 EM radiation can be extremely **useful**.

a) Using the boxes below, number the following types of EM radiation in order of **decreasing** frequency (1 = highest frequency). Write down one use for each type of radiation.

☐ Ultraviolet ....

☐ X-rays ....

☐ Infrared ....

b) Low-intensity light can be used for **iris scanning**. Write down one advantage and one disadvantage of using iris scanning as a form of identification.

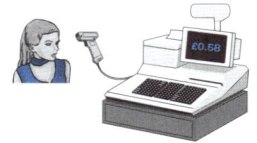

Advantage: ....

Disadvantage: ....

c) Radio waves from space can be monitored for signs of extraterrestrial intelligence. Are radio waves transverse or longitudinal? ....

Q2 It's not currently safe to send **humans** to other planets. Circle the correct word in each pair to complete the following passage about other ways to **investigate** our Solar System.

> **Robots** / **Animals** can be sent to collect samples from the surfaces of planets.
>
> However, landing spacecraft on other planets is difficult and expensive, so a lot of
>
> research is done by **spatial** / **remote** sensing. A spacecraft can be sent into orbit
>
> around the planet, where it **records** / **transmits** information using data-loggers.
>
> Radio waves or **ultrasound** / **microwaves** can be used to send the data back to Earth.

Q3 The Sun is roughly halfway through its **stable phase**.

a) Tick the boxes to show whether the statements below are true or false.

	True	False
A star in its stable phase is called a 'main stage star'.	☐	☐
At the end of its stable phase, the Sun will become a red giant.	☐	☐
The Sun will eventually become a neutron star.	☐	☐
There are no heavy elements in the Sun.	☐	☐

b) Explain why planets can sometimes be seen in the night sky, despite not producing their own light.

....

Q4 Steve is looking at Venus from Earth. If EM waves travel at 3×10^8 **m/s** and light from Venus takes **200 seconds** to reach Steve, calculate the **distance** between Venus and Earth.

....

Mixed Questions — P1b Topics 11 & 12

Q5 Comets are made of dust and ice.

a) Why do comets often have tails?

....

b) Comets are visible because light from the Sun is **reflected** off them. When this light enters the atmosphere, it gets **refracted**, because the atmosphere is denser than space.
Complete the ray diagram to show what happens.
(Assume the atmosphere's density is the same throughout.)

Remember to draw the 'normal'.

George was going down.

Atmosphere

Earth

Q6 A space probe is sent to **remotely** observe Mars.

a) The probe has a mass of 3200 kg and is accelerating at 9.2 m/s². Calculate the **force** on the probe.

....

b) The probe sends **analogue** radio signals back to Earth.
The signals have a frequency of 95.6 MHz.

i) Calculate the wavelength of the radio signals. (Use $v = 3 \times 10^8$ m/s.)

....

ii) Describe the main difference between an analogue and a digital signal.

....

Think about the 'values' of the signal.

....

c) When the signal reaches a receiver on Earth, it is sent to a network of computers through **optical fibres**. What **two** types of EM wave can be used in optical fibres?

....

d) So far, there have been no manned missions to Mars. Write down one of the **ill effects** such a long space flight could have on astronauts and suggest how this could be **reduced**.

....

e) The **acceleration due to gravity** on Mars is about 4 N/kg (as opposed to about 10 N/kg on Earth) If, in the future, an 80 kg astronaut is sent to Mars, what will their **weight** be on the surface?

....